Power and Care

Power and Care

Toward Balance for Our Common Future—Science, Society, and Spirituality

edited by Tania Singer and Matthieu Ricard with Kate Karius

with contributions by His Holiness the Dalai Lama

The MIT Press
Cambridge, Massachusetts
London, England

© 2018 Allary Éditions

Published by special arrangement with Allary Éditions in conjunction with their duly appointed agent 2 Seas Literary Agency.

This book was set in Stone Serif by Westchester Publishing Services. Printed and bound in the United States of America.

Library of Congress Cataloging-in-Publication Data is available.

ISBN: 978-0-262-03952-9

10 9 8 7 6 5 4 3 2 1

Contents

Foreword

THE DALAI LAMA

I am very pleased that this meeting on Power and Care, the second to be organized by Mind & Life Europe, has taken place in Brussels.

This initiative started more than 30 years ago when my good friend, the late neuroscientist Francisco Varela, led a group of scientists to Dharamsala for our first discussions.

Today, these dialogues continue to be of mutual benefit to Tibetan Buddhist scholars and scientists alike, as well as anyone interested in creating a better humanity.

27 January 2018

Introduction

Tania Singer and Matthieu Ricard, Content Curators
of the Power and Care Dialogue

One of the great problems of history is that the concepts of love and power have usually been contrasted as opposites, polar opposites. ... Power at its best is love implementing the demands of justice, and justice at its best is power correcting everything that stands against love.

—Martin Luther King, Jr., August 16, 1967

A Call for Care in a Challenging World

Our world today is full of challenges. Around our planet, events, including the conflicts in the Middle East, the refugee crisis, crumbling governments, and economies nearing bankruptcy, alert us to a world in distress. At the societal level, we are experiencing poverty in the midst of plenty, increasing inequality gaps, racism, resource depletion, and climate change. On the individual level, the number of stress-related diseases, feelings of uncertainty, depression, and loneliness, and exaggerated expressions of individualism and narcissism are on the rise.

While inspiring initiatives and innovations—from the United Nations' Sustainable Development Goals and the Paris Agreement on Climate Change to great works of care and determination and an increase in social media—unite us as global citizens of a shared planet, for many of us, it is still difficult to find ways to take responsibility to create a more sustainable and just world.[1] Questions remain, including these: How can we overcome our planet's daunting challenges? How can we become more responsible and caring global citizens? How can we go beyond our own selfish tendencies and widen our circles of compassion to care not only about our nearest kin, friends, or members of the same nation or religion but also about those foreign to us, other species, and the environment at large?

Dialogues to Increase Human Well-being

For the past thirty years, His Holiness the Dalai Lama has been involved with world researchers to support pathways for knowledge to increase human well-being, ethical responsibility, and compassion.

Dialogues with the Dalai Lama initially started as small, privately held scientific meetings, which led in 1987 to the creation of the Mind & Life Institute, a charitable, nonprofit organization founded by the 14th Dalai Lama, neuroscientist Francisco Varela, and entrepreneur Adam Engle. The purpose of the Mind & Life Institute is to create open dialogue and research collaboration between modern sciences, the world's living contemplative traditions, philosophy, the humanities, and the social sciences.

Over the years, the Mind & Life Institute events have become more frequent, accessible, and widely publicized. In 2008, the organization expanded into Europe, and Mind & Life Europe was established. Furthering the mission of the Mind & Life Institute, Mind & Life Europe serves to alleviate suffering and promote flourishing by developing contemplative science on the European continent.

About Power and Care

In September 2016, Mind & Life Europe held its second dialogue in Europe, and Mind & Life's 31st public dialogue with the Dalai Lama. Taking place in Brussels, Belgium, the capital of the European Union, this three-day dialogue was the largest Mind & Life conference to date.[2] At the event, 19 leading experts came together with His Holiness the Dalai Lama to examine the two fundamental forces of power and care within the framework of the current state of our planet. Because power and care manifest in both the natural and social realms, these discussions explore how to best combine and balance these forces across a wide variety of disciplines including anthropology, ethology, psychology, neuroscience, economics, governance, social activism, and the world's contemplative traditions.

Introducing the Concepts of Power and Care

The notion of power is a neutral concept that is neither harmful nor beneficial by nature and supports us in achieving our goals. Yet, the Western historical and psychological perspective often links power to concepts such as domination, instrumentalization, or sovereignty. This idea of "power over someone" is an aspect in the broad concept of power, apparent in political, societal, and interpersonal spheres, as indicated by problems such as the wealth gap and racial and gender inequality, among others. But power is essentially a motivational *force* that can be used to benefit others or to harm them, to build or to destroy. What we make of this force lies in our intention.

Similarly, care is another important motivational *force*. Yet, unlike power, it is not ethically neutral, as it aims at increasing the well-being of others, be it our next of kin or society at large. Care evokes concepts such as altruism, compassion, cooperation, responsibility, and affiliation. Care, at first sight, may not be perceived as being compatible with power, but this is not the case. Power, imbued with care, can achieve much more for the good of others than a powerless motivation to care, and power, without the intention to benefit others and the common good, can become ruthless and unethical.

Overview of the Book

This book recounts the discussions that took place at the BOZAR Centre for Fine Arts in Brussels, September 9–11, 2016. While the material has been edited for content and clarity, this book is a faithful representation of the events as they took place. In the following pages, you will be introduced to world-renowned scholars from diverse disciplines, and their focus of study, as seen through the perspective of power and care. You will glean insight on the Dalai Lama's responses to these presentations, as well as comments from the sessions' moderators and other presenters.

His Holiness the Dalai Lama participated in every session together with his longtime English translator, Thupten Jinpa. While His Holiness follows and articulates complex scientific and philosophical arguments in English, he sometimes chooses to speak in Tibetan. When this occurred during the conference, Jinpa would translate what His Holiness said into English. In this book, we have represented this translated speech as His Holiness's own words.

Tracking the event's five panels, the book is divided into five parts. Each part includes an introduction to the content, and the chapters within each part constitute individual presentations. The chapters appear in the same order in which they occurred.

Part I, Perspectives from Ethology, Anthropology, and Ecology, provides insights about power and care in our closest relatives, the chimpanzees. Good leadership includes a healthy dose of care, which is why alpha males are often consoling others. Similarly, in early humans, care is one of the most powerful instincts and is the biological basis for altruism extended to non-related individuals. In our early history, care was important for developing empathy and autonomy. This part also explores the expansion of human civilization, where we existed as equalitarian and cooperative hunter-gatherers for more than 95% of the time, and the fact that we have reached an era where human beings have gained the power to dramatically alter the state of the planet. Unless drastic measures are taken, we are moving toward the sixth major extinction since life appeared on Earth, bringing an end to thousands of known and unknown species and creating immense suffering and destruction for future generations. Yet, today, we have the technological know-how to avoid this catastrophe. What we lack is the will and conviction to set the already existing solutions into action.

Part II, Perspectives from Psychology, Endocrinology, and Neuroscience, shares that the potential for inner change and plasticity is possible by gearing our intentions so that we can directly influence our behavior and interactions. Power and care motives are covered, as well as the ability to transform power to care by purposefully going into the shadows of one's personality to create more space for love. This ability to transform is also provided through recent research in the fields of social and contemplative neurosciences, which shows that, through short, disciplined, meditation-based mental training programs, human qualities such as mindfulness, altruism, compassion, and perspective taking can be cultivated and trained. These practices not only lead to specific changes in the brain but also support stress-reduction, improved health and immune system functions, greater happiness and well-being, and increased prosocial behavior and cooperation. The latest neuroscience is offered, providing insight into the hormones and neurotransmitters associated with these motivational systems. Oxytocin, the hormone most closely associated with care, has been shown to mediate trust, bonding, and affiliative and prosocial behaviors. The hormone testosterone, which is frequently linked to power and aggressive behaviors, has also been shown to increase certain helping behaviors, particularly if they lead to an increase in one's own status and reputation.

In part III, Perspectives from Spiritual and Religious Traditions, insight into the overarching message of all major religions, love, is shared by theistic and nontheistic religious leaders. This message of love is also expressed in indigenous cultures by caring for Mother Earth. The imbalance of power and care within the realm of religion is addressed, which is rooted in the recent emergence of power in religion as seen through acts of coercion, violence, and destruction in the quest to convert others.

Perspectives from Economics and Society, part IV, highlights the ability to cultivate our mind and heart to change self-centered, selfish motivations to more caring and affiliative ones that promote prosocial behavior and global cooperation. This is crucial in building more sustainable societies that work cooperatively toward common goals. Recent events, including the financial crisis, are discussed, as well as the emergence of more realistic, inclusive, and empirically founded economic and organizational models that involve notions of sustainability and care. These have the potential to redesign our educational, economic, and political institutions, businesses and laws, and also greatly impact our own lives.

Lastly, in part V, Personal Commitment and Global Responsibility, works of art and activism—from allowing art to express concepts that are too complex to comprehend, to business plans for peace, and the emergence of new organizations that work like living organisms over machines—are highlighted. These are especially important in helping to create a society of more responsible and caring citizens, where all voices are recognized and heard, and help to widen the circle of compassion. By cultivating care and altruism within each one of us, and in society, we can reach our natural potential for kindness and cooperation and use these forces for their highest good.

Creating a More Compassionate World

Through exploration into the forces of power and care, which shape human development on both the individual and collective levels, these dialogues serve to stimulate ideas on how these forces can be conscientiously and fruitfully allied.

It is Mind & Life's hope that this book will inspire readers and compassionate actors everywhere. We hope it will also serve as a significant catalyst for the formulation of new research ideas and projects, and for imagining societal and governance structures and leadership practices that promote the flourishing of living beings and our planet.

Notes

1. In 2015, the General Assembly of the United Nations adopted the 17 Sustainable Development Goals (SDGs) to be achieved by 2030. Among the 17 sustainable goals, let us mention, for example: ending poverty and hunger, ensuring inclusive and quality education for all, access to water and sanitation for all, achieving gender equality and empowering women and girls, and so on.

2. In fulfilling this mission, at the Power and Care conference, over 2,000 participants were in attendance, and nearly 900 tickets were either given away or sold at a reduced price to support a younger generation of leaders and scientists.

I Perspectives from Ethology, Anthropology, and Ecology

This first session starts with an Opening Address by His Holiness the Dalai Lama. Afterward, a very big picture on the concepts of power and care is provided by looking at the complex interactions of these forces in primates with Frans de Waal. Through the early ages of human history up to the present, Sarah Blaffer Hrdy shares how humans have a unique way to offer maternal and paternal care for their offspring and to mutually care for one another. Lastly, Johan Rockström reveals the impact of power and care on the current state of our planet and on the fate of future generations.

—Matthieu Ricard, Ph.D., first-session moderator, a Buddhist monk at the Shechen Monastery in Nepal, humanitarian, writer, and photographer

Opening Address

His Holiness the Dalai Lama

I am very pleased that this Mind & Life meeting on Power and Care has taken place in Brussels on the European continent.

My first visit to Europe was in 1973. I recognized on this trip that European countries are materially highly developed, through technology and modern science. I also realized on this visit that the people who enjoy these conveniences were not necessarily happy. They suffered from too much stress and competition, which creates, in particular, jealousy. This led me to feel that material development is certainly a provider of physical comfort, but not of mental comfort.

Through material development alone, there is no guarantee of being a happy person or having a happy family. Therefore, in order to tackle mental-level problems, including the abuse of drugs and alcohol, which serve to provide temporary comfort, one has to look to the mind.

Since the eighth century, Tibetans have been learning about ancient Indian knowledge, including psychology, and we have held onto this knowledge for over a thousand years through rigorous study and practice. Our knowledge about the mind and emotions is thus highly developed.

During this first trip to Europe, I felt that sharing this ancient knowledge might contribute to inner peace, irrespective of whether one is a believer or a nonbeliever. After all, we are all human beings—we are physically, emotionally, and mentally the same. We all want a happy life ... and when we say a happy life, we should not forget inner peace. This is what eventually led to the start of the Mind & Life Dialogues.

Dialogues to Seek Answers through Investigation and Experimentation

When I started meeting with modern scientists, some senior monks, scholars, and others initially had reservations. They felt the science that comes from the West was far too closed-minded and involved some danger. One person even warned me, "A dialogue with a scientist is quite a serious matter, so be careful. Science is a killer of religion."

I then reflected on the words that Buddha taught his followers: "Monks and scholars should not accept my teaching out of faith, or out of devotion, but rather out of investigation and experimentation." So, I felt there was no problem. Skepticism is essential in order to carry out an investigation, in order to find out the reality or an answer. If you believe something, then there are no questions, and without a question, there is no incentive to investigate.

This led me to conclude that, in general, scientific inquiry and Buddha's teaching, particularly in the Nalanda tradition, are similar: to investigate with an unbiased attitude and an open mind.

Learnings of Mutual Benefit

I have mentioned that, thanks to the Indian Buddhist heritage—especially of Nalanda University—the Tibetan tradition has accumulated a lot of ancient knowledge.[1] And while ancient Indian Buddhist literature mentions particles and atoms, the theory of how the material world is composed of the five elements, and the fact that everything comes from and dissolves into space—the scientific research findings shared at these dialogues have been of immense help to us Buddhist scholars.[2]

At these events, by sharing the knowledge we have developed and held onto for centuries, Western scientists also obtain useful information about the mind and methods to tackle destructive emotions. So, by strictly following a nonreligious approach, we can learn from each other about the nature of reality and our shared human condition.

Europeans—Learning from the Past and Leading for the Future

Here on the European continent, I am often told that, over many centuries, there was a lot of fighting and killing. In the 20th century, there was the First World War, and then the Second World War. During these wars, tremendous acts of violence took place. According to history, 100 million people were killed.

Now, in the 21st century, humans may still often feel some sense of disagreement, and the immediate response is to think about how to resolve this by force. Unfortunately, today, even religious groups are creating divisions, making religion itself a cause for more killing. Yet, all religion teaches us the oneness of humanity. According to the theistic religions, all 7.5 billion humans have been created by God, and according to the nontheistic religions, we all are the same—sentient beings who want peace or happiness.

Historically, this continent has been involved in violence and war, and the European people have experienced a lot of suffering. This has led the continent to also become more mature. In the past, one factor that contributed to this violence was too much emphasis on "my" nation, "their" nation. Now, Modern Europe has created this European Union.

In the 1990s, on one occasion, when he was also in his nineties, my late and very close friend—who I also considered my tutor about quantum physics—Carl Friedrich von Weizsäcker told me that when he was a young German, in every French eye, Germany was the enemy. Similarly, in German eyes, France was the enemy. This kind of attitude has now completely changed. This recognition of inner values, which include compassion, tolerance, self-discipline, and knowing how to be content, is an indication of progress and development. Similarly, in America, a number of people, including some institutions, universities, and even cities, are now showing interest in inner peace through the practice of love and compassion.

Today, this continent, with the European Union, has a good basis to work from. I am sure that Europe can lead this work to bring a happier life to humanity that includes material comfort, physical comfort, and inner development with full knowledge about our mind and our emotions. Then, you see, inner peace can be attained. This is my wish and my hope.

Notes

1. Nalanda was the most famous Buddhist university of ancient India. It was founded at the beginning of the 2nd century CE and became the major center for philosophical and spiritual studies of Asia, attracting scholars from many other countries as

far as China, Mongolia, Sri Lanka, and so on. It remained as such until the end of the 12th century CE or beginning of the 13th century. It was then destroyed by the Muslim armies led by Muhamad Khilji. Nalanda University teachers include famous Buddhist philosophers such as Asanga, Vasubandhu, and Nagarjuna.

2. According to the *Abhidharma*, one of the most important texts on Buddhist philosophy, the five elements are: earth, water, fire, air, and ether.

1 The Power and Care of Primate Alpha Males

Frans B. M. De Waal

Your Holiness, in my work as a primatologist and ethologist, I have studied chimpanzees—one of our closest relatives—throughout my life. This has led me to assume that the concepts of power and care also apply to them.

Chimpanzee Politics

"Chimpanzee politics" is a term that we use to describe the social complexity of apes[1] in relation to power and dominance. The reason we call it "politics" is because it is not automatically the biggest and strongest male who is the dominant male: the alpha male. It can actually be the smallest male who is dominant.

Dominance is entirely based on coalitions. It is based on the answers to these questions: "Do you have support from the females? Do you have support from other males?" Being an alpha male also means that you need to keep your supporters happy. Otherwise, they will stop backing you. So, it is really like a political system. Physical strength is important, but it is not the only element that decides.

Displaying Power and Dominance in Chimpanzees

The body language of dominance is very clear in chimpanzees. These two adult males are both the same size, but the one on the left is the dominant male (figure 1.1). He demonstrates his position by walking upright with a bipedal swagger and by putting all of his hair up to look impressive. The chimpanzee on the right shows submission by bowing and grunting.

Figure 1.1
There is very clear body language for displaying dominance and subordinance in chimpanzees.
Photo: Frans B. M. de Waal

Displaying Power and Dominance in Human Beings

Similarly, in the human species, body language also makes it extremely clear who is dominant and who is subordinate and is shown in a way that is not much different from chimpanzees. As seen in politicians and royalty, dominant humans also display a bipedal swagger, make themselves look large, sit on a throne, and so on. If you walk into a corporate boardroom with 25 people, you will know within 30 seconds who the dominant person is just by his or her body language.

Studies in Empathy and Consolation Behavior

With regard to care, I would like to share some examples from our recent studies on empathy and consolation behavior in a number of species. Empathy, as defined in the dictionary, is the ability to understand and share the feelings of another. From this explanation, you can see the two components: understanding, which is the cognitive component, and feeling, the emotional component. We most often study the emotional component of empathy when we look at animals by asking questions like "Are they in tune with each other's emotions?" And all mammals are. The reason most people have cats and dogs at home, and not lizards or fish, is because humans like mammals. We enjoy the emotional exchange we have with them. They understand our emotions, and we understand theirs.

Recently, an enormous amount of evidence has been accumulated on all sorts of mammals with regard to empathy. In a study that we conducted on voles—a small rodent that is similar to a mouse—we learned that their neuroscience of consolation behavior is very similar to the human neuroscience of empathy. The act of consolation expressed is calming body contact, which is aimed at a distressed individual.

In a similar study, we looked at consolation in bonobos at the Lola ya Bonobo Sanctuary, near Kinshasa, in the Democratic Republic of the Congo, Africa. As chimpanzees, bonobos are closely related to us. When a bonobo loses a fight, another may approach and provide reassurance, or what we call consolation. This is their main expression of empathy. Bonobos and chimpanzees show frequent consolation behavior, whereas a lot of other primates, such as monkeys, do not always display such acts of empathy.

It is important to highlight that the bonobos in this sanctuary are traumatized orphans. As victims of the bush meat trade, these apes are most often confiscated from the market when they are babies and raised by humans. Because of this, most of the bonobos in the sanctuary have an abnormal upbringing. Yet, there are a few mother-raised bonobos in the sanctuary as well, which I would like to talk about.

In the graph shown in figure 1.2, which highlights consolation behavior and its level of frequency, you can see that the young bonobos in the sanctuary provide more consolation than adults. Most likely, this is because adults become more selective in whom they provide consolation to as they mature. The young display consolation to almost everyone while the older bonobos display consolation only to their family, friends, and so on. If you look at the mother-reared bonobos, they show far more consolation than everybody else (the only mother-reared bonobos in this study were juveniles.)

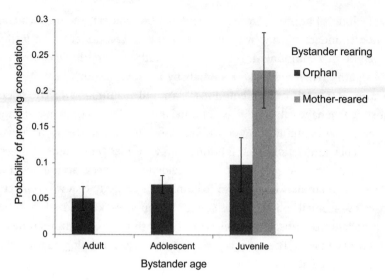

Figure 1.2
The effect of bystander age and rearing on the probability of providing consolation
to victims of aggression at the Lola ya Bonobo Sanctuary. The graph provides the
mean±SEM proportion of conflicts per individual to which they were bystander.
Source: Z. Clay and F. B. M. de Waal, "Bonobos Respond to Distress in Others: Consolation across the Age Spectrum," *PLOS One* 8 (2013): e5520.

Empathy Studies in Human Beings

The first studies of human empathy were also studies on consolation.
Family members were asked to cry, and scientists looked at how children
responded. Young children, even two-year-olds, would walk up to, touch,
and stroke the family member to provide consolation as an act of empathy.
In human children, girls provide more consolation than boys. Universally,
empathy is higher in female mammals than in male mammals.

Lack of an ability to console has been found in humans as well. For
instance, studies with traumatized human orphans in Romania reveal very
low levels of empathy. These children have a very disturbed emotional
life. In the case of the unmothered bonobos, we also see this same process
going on.

What Constitutes a Good Leader?

When we think about leadership and the combination of power and care, we tend to think that the most dominant male in a chimpanzee group must be a bully, that he must reap all the benefits and not do much otherwise—but that is not really how it works. Just as in humans, in chimpanzees, there are two types of alpha males: dictators and good leaders.

In chimpanzees, a good leader is someone who keeps the peace. In figure 1.3, you see an alpha male who is standing between fighting females. He intervenes to stop the fighting between them, and a good alpha male does this frequently. Alpha males, when they are good leaders, stop fights, even the smallest fights between two kids. It is very important, because if you do not stop the fighting between kids, then their mothers start fighting. I hear that at daycare centers, this is not so unusual. This makes the ability to stop the fights a very important task. A good alpha male also protects the weak

Figure 1.3
An alpha male, intervening to keep the peace.
Photo: Frans B. M. de Waal

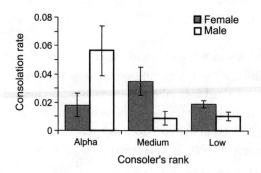

Figure 1.4
Alpha males are the top consolers. The graph shows the rate of consolation (mean±SEM) offered to distressed others corrected for the total number of opportunities in relation to the sex and rank of consolers.
Source: M. T. Romero, M. A. Castellanos, and F. B. M. de Waal, "Consolation as Possible Expression of Sympathetic Concern among Chimpanzees," *Proceedings of the National Academy of Sciences, USA* 107 (2010): 12110–12115.

and becomes very popular as a result. Good leaders also provide consolation, and thousands of my case studies reveal this.

In the graph shown in figure 1.4, the rate of consolation according to sex is displayed, which shows that females provide more consolation to distressed individuals than males. But among the males there is one exception. The graph also shows that the alpha male provides far more consolation than anyone else.

Attributes of a Popular Alpha Male: Peacemaker and Consoler-in-Chief

In summary, the alpha male not only keeps the peace in the group. He is also the main provider of consolation for individuals who are in trouble or have been beaten up. While there are some alpha males who rule by force and terror, many more alpha males are caring leaders. A popular alpha male is one who needs support, gets support, and is supported by the group; otherwise, he would probably not be an alpha male. He is a peacemaker and the consoler-in-chief.

The Dalai Lama: Biological matters are wonderful! We are social animals. Naturally, we love affection; it is a major factor in bringing us together. People sometimes consider the practice of love and compassion to be part of a religious practice. This leads people to think that people who have no interest in world religion have no interest in love and compassion, and this is totally wrong. I believe that, in themselves, qualities like love and compassion are independent of religion. They are fundamental human qualities and relate to values that are universal.

Your explanation is very good, particularly with regard to females' being more sensitive about others' behavior. With chimpanzees, or any other animal, there is no record that they start war, apart from some infighting. Yet, for humans, war is part of our history. Why? Chimpanzees are stronger, at least their hands are much stronger than ours, yet there is no sort of intelligence on how to manipulate or how to defeat. Only human beings have the ability to create things like nuclear weapons. No other animal does this. To tackle these human-made problems requires us to combine our warmheartedness with our intelligence, so that we can become more constructive. Otherwise, we can become destructive, when our intelligence is combined with anger and hatred.

Frans de Waal: The European Union, or the EU, was formed after World War II as a political pact. It is now an economic pact, but it was intended to bring France and Germany together on the reasoning that if you increase the value of the relationship so that the countries need each other, you can reduce the chance of conflict between them.

A pact is very much something that happens in primates. I have done studies throughout my career on reconciliation and peacemaking in primates, and we call this the valuable relationship hypothesis. You can experimentally increase the value of relationships between, let us say, two monkeys, by allowing them to get food only if they work together. If you then induce conflict, you will notice that the monkeys will reconcile much more easily. Mutual dependence is a big actor in preventing warfare, and it can be demonstrated in animals. You do not need religion, and you do not necessarily need politics. You can show it in animals. They understand.

The Dalai Lama: You used the word: "chimpanzee politics."

Frans de Waal: Yes, but you do not necessarily need that kind of thinking, because a lot of animals are mutually dependent and attached, which is a very strong mechanism for preventing aggression. The EU is based on that principle.

Note

1. Ethologists have established a clear difference between monkeys and great apes. Apes, belonging to the hominid family, share various characteristics that differentiate them from monkeys (also called "lesser apes"), such as: a more developed brain imbued with more sophisticated cognitive abilities, a greater height and weight, no tail, and arms that are longer than the legs. Chimpanzees, bonobos, gorillas, and orangutans are among the best-known species of apes.

2   The Transformative Power of Nurturing

Sarah Blaffer Hrdy

Your Holiness, I would like to discuss the transformative power of nurturing and how it can help explain processes by which apes in the line leading to the genus *Homo*, our line, became even more empathetic and more interested in what others are thinking and feeling than the closely related apes that Frans De Waal just told you about. My question is "How can we use what evolutionary anthropologists are learning about human origins to encourage the powerful to be more caring?"

Care in Early Human Origins

The closest proxies we humans have to our last common ancestor with other apes are extant great apes such as chimpanzees. As with humans, in chimpanzees there is a close bond between mother and offspring, but with an important difference. After giving birth, the extraordinarily possessive chimpanzee mother will not allow her baby out of touch for a single moment, day or night, for months (see figure 2.1). In turn, her infant clings to her like his or her life depends on it, and it does. A chimpanzee continues to suckle her baby for half a decade, but once weaned, her baby is nutritionally self-sufficient. No one else helps to feed him or her.

By contrast, among hunter-gatherers—people still rearing their children much as our Pleistocene ancestors must have—mothers allow and even encourage others to hold their newborn (see figure 2.2). A child remains dependent on both his mother *and on others* for many years.[1]

One reason for this striking difference is that a chimpanzee mother cannot trust the adults around her not to harm her infant while hunter-gatherer mothers usually can. Secondly, the hunter-gatherer mother is aware that help from others will be essential for her baby's survival. Do not

Figure 2.1
After birth, the highly protective and possessive chimpanzee mother holds her infant
in direct skin-to-skin contact for months.
Photo: Jutta Hof

mistake me, mothers are critically important. But as among African forag-
ing people today, a baby born among our ancestors would have spent much
of his or her first day of life being held by allomothers—females or males
other than the mother (see figure 2.3).

Hunter-Gatherer Parenting: Help from Others Is Essential for Survival

Allomothers can be older siblings, grandmothers, fathers, aunts, cousins,
and maybe even another woman. Should this other woman be lactating,
she might briefly suckle the baby. Hunter-gatherer babies are weaned earlier
than other apes, and as weaning approaches, allomothers help with provisioning by delivering premasticated food and other treats. This is important
because evidence from people still living by hunting and gathering when
first studied by anthropologists indicates that infants with the most caretakers at age one were most likely to survive to age three. It is no wonder
that infants with the most caregivers are most likely to survive. Almost

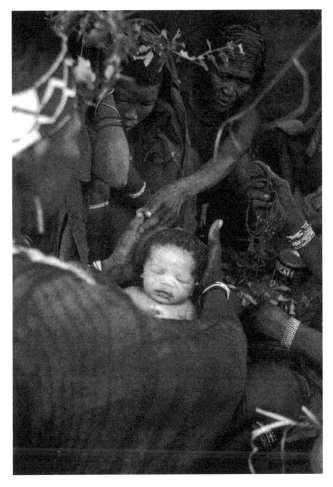

Figure 2.2
This hunter-gatherer mother has just given birth and hands her baby to her own mother to massage the baby's scalp while other group members gather around, awaiting their turn to hold the baby.
Photo: Marjorie Shostak/Anthro-Photo

Figure 2.3
In this artistic reconstruction of *Homo erectus* living in Africa two million years ago, a mother hands her baby to an allomother; in this instance, an older sibling.
Art by: Viktor Deak/Copyright SBH Lit.

no other mammal produces offspring that mature more slowly, and none produce offspring that are more costly. Once weaned, other apes provision themselves, but little humans remain dependent for 15 to 20 years, requiring supplementary foods provided by other group members.[2]

Allomaternal Assistance Helped Fuel Costly Brains

It takes 13 million calories to raise an infant from birth to when that child is producing as much as he or she consumes, yet hunter-gatherer children are weaned earlier. Shorter intervals between births mean that a mother is likely to be pregnant with or already nursing another baby long before her older child is independent.[3] These combined demands would be greater than what a mother by herself could meet.[4] Over the course of the Pleistocene, energetic demands from growing and maintaining increasingly costly sapient brains magnified the challenge of keeping slow-maturing offspring nourished. Brains are energetically expensive organs to grow and maintain, and they doubled in size from 450 cubic centimeters among our last common ancestors with other apes and australopithecines to over 900 cubic centimeters by two million years ago.

By the emergence of *Homo sapiens*, brains had evolved to some 1,350 cubic centimeters. Furthermore, scientists are just learning that the metabolic demand for human brains does not peak until 4 to 5 years of age, which would be after a hunter-gatherer child had been weaned.[5] Extra energy to fuel these big brains had to come from somewhere. This made group members, other than the mother, who were willing to share, essential.

The Importance of Shared Care and Provisioning

The challenges of sustaining dependent children would have been further magnified by Pleistocene African climates, which were characterized by unpredictable rainfall and recurring droughts. Even with more meat in the diet, hunting is a very unreliable way to make a living. Studies of modern African hunter-gatherers reveal that hunters are only occasionally successful, and overall, men bring in only 40% of the calories required. The remaining 60% of calories come from more reliably obtained plant foods gathered by women. A critical portion of shared foods is obtained by grandmothers and other older women past child-rearing age (see figure 2.4).[6]

I agree with the anthropologist Kristen Hawkes and her colleagues that the most plausible explanation for why—unlike other apes—women go on living for decades after they can no longer reproduce had to do with the critical roles postmenopausal women played among our ancestors, by helping to care for and especially provision younger kin. Longer postmenopausal survival was just one of the evolutionary implications of humankind's deep history of shared care and provisioning. But the message is clear: there is no way on Darwin's Earth that humans could have emerged unless mothers had had a lot of help.

Figure 2.4
A 62-year-old Hazda great-aunt moves a boulder to get at the starchy tubers buried underneath. Her own children have all died, and she is collecting food for her sister's children.
Photo: Courtesy of James O'Connell and Kristen Hawkes

Infants Are Conditioned to Attend to What Others Intend

I believe that this need for allomaternal assistance had profound implications for mothers who had to become increasingly sensitive to how much social support they were likely to have. It also had implications for infants, who grew up dependent on others and needed to rely on them. Developmental psychologists have learned that both human babies and nonhuman ape infants reared in captivity spend more time looking into the faces of others and monitoring their eye gaze when they are held by someone else a short distance away from their mothers.[7] By six months of age, ancestral human babies accustomed to being held by others began to spontaneously engage in attention-getting behaviors like babbling. Group members rewarded such engaging behaviors by paying attention, providing soft food treats, and generally conditioning babies to initiate more such contacts.[8]

For years, psychologists have been aware that children with older siblings are better at mentalizing, what is called "Theory of Mind."[9] Those with multiple attachment figures early on exhibit improved social skills later in life.[10] Even before they can talk, little humans are interested in ingratiating themselves with others. Toddlers spontaneously share, and they even pick out a piece of food to offer to someone else that is different from their own preference, if they think that person will like it.[11] Engaging in this kind of behavior makes them happy.[12]

Multiple Caretakers Promote Intersubjective Engagement

Having multiple caretakers is also correlated with enhanced capacities to integrate multiple perspectives.[13] Such children care what others are thinking and are better at taking into account what someone else knows when they try to communicate. Over the course of development, they grow up so as to feel pride when approved of, and shame when disapproved of. Those children, who are just a little better at learning to ingratiate themselves with others and soliciting nurture, would be those best cared for and best fed. Over generations, and over evolutionary time, these would also have been the youngsters most likely to survive, favored by Darwinian natural selection.[14] At the same time, their caretakers were also being transformed.

Psychobiological Responses in Caretakers

As we look at a cute baby, our reward centers in the orbital frontal cortex are stimulated.[15] Whether women or men, parents or alloparents, people respond to babies.[16] Profound psychophysiological changes can be documented in fathers who are engaged in caretaking. Prolactin levels rise above previous baselines while testosterone levels decline. There may also be surges in oxytocin—a neuropeptide typically associated with giving birth, the let-down reflex during lactation, or female orgasms. Elicitors of these responses include infantile cries or other signals of need and may vary depending on how much prior caretaking experience the man has had and his relationship with the mother, as well as his probable genetic relatedness. But the key factor is prolonged, intimate contact with babies. Fathers' brains show many of the same neuroendocrine responses as mothers'. Even an adopted baby stimulates such surges in oxytocin, so long as the foster father is intimately involved in nurturing that baby.[17] In other words, alloparents and parents alike undergo similar neuroendocrine responses.

When my first grandchild was born, I wondered how I would respond. Just before meeting him for the first time, I took a sample of my own saliva. Two hours later, I took another sample. There was a 63% surge in my oxytocin levels. When my husband arrived, even before I gave him a hug, I handed him a tube and said, "Spit here, dear." After two hours of holding his grandson, his oxytocin level went up a little bit. By the second day, after another two hours, Grand-Dad's oxytocin levels had surged to the same level as mine had (see figure 2.5).

So, if I am right, by two million years ago when *Homo erectus* was emerging, our ancestors were already beginning to share care and provisioning. This means that long before humans became the brainiest, the smartest, and the most enculturated apes, and long before sophisticated human language, we were already the most caring and other-regarding apes.

Can the Powerful Become More Caring?

My question, Your Holiness, is "Might we find ways to tap these ancient potentials for nurture so integral to the human species in order to motivate the powerful to be more caring?"

I am reminded of an intervention recently undertaken in Rio de Janeiro, Brazil. An order came to clear out the local favelas. In the process, some policemen were accused of shooting street urchins. In response, someone had the inspired idea to tap into the transformative power of nurture by sending the flak-jacket-wearing burly policemen into daycare centers, to spend time holding and caring for babies. Possibly, through this exposure, ancient emotional potentials could be reenlisted (see figure 2.6). I hope it worked.

The Dalai Lama: On one occasion with scientists, I was told about a series of experiments which revealed that, basically, human nature is more compassionate and caring. A compassionate mind means to take care. This is logical because we are social animals. As mentioned, for at least a few years, our survival is entirely dependent on others' care. So, that is nature: our nature.

At a meeting in Hawaii, one scientist shared this about turtles: The mother comes, lays her eggs, and leaves. When the young turtles hatch,

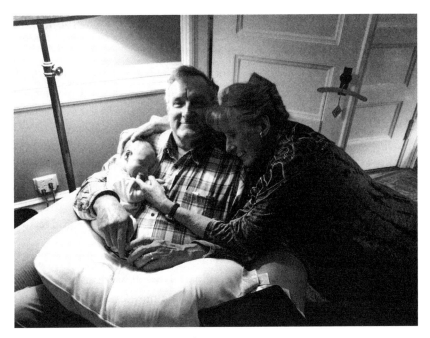

Figure 2.5
Ephemeral surges in oxytocin levels similar to those reported for mothers, fathers, and adoptive parents also occur in grandparents following prolonged intimate contact with a new baby.
Photo: Katrinka Hrdy

Figure 2.6
Rio de Janeiro policemen sensitized to be more caring through intimate contact with babies.
Photo: Lalo de Almeida/The New York Times/Redux

they have to start off and fight on their own to survive. If an egg is marked, and the mother is kept nearby, when the turtle hatches, and the mother and the youngster are reunited, there will not be any sign of affection. That is nature: the turtle's survival is not dependent on its mother's care.

Conversely, in humans, even during the time in utero, a mother's affectionate mind is a very crucial and positive factor in the health of an unborn child while a mother's fear and anger can have a very bad effect. Scientists have told me that even after birth, a mother's physical touch is critical for the proper enlargement of the baby's brain. These are the biological factors of human nature.

Basic human nature is compassionate. If you are caring, and if you make an effort, there is real hope. If basic human nature is aggressive and angry, then there is no hope. Then, I think we should pray for the elimination of humanity on this planet. (Laughter.)

Children at a young age are naturally compassionate; their human nature is more alive. They live together, play together, and do not care about difference of color, religion, or nationality. Gradually, though, as we grow up and enter into the educational system, problems come. This is because we do not receive sufficient information about the importance of compassion. This creates power in a negative sense—physical power, economic power, political power—which leads us to start to make divisions and distinctions on the basis of color, religion, and nationality. Eventually, we start to make distinctions within the same nationality, and even within the same faith: rich or poor, influential or uninfluential. We also learn to calculate: "This person is someone influential" or "If I make a friendship with him or her, I will gain more."

This problem exists because our existing educational system does not pay attention to our deeper inner values. Usually, we say, "A healthy mind, a healthy body," and while there is a close connection, most of us only focus on having a healthy body. We do not pay enough attention to having a healthier mind. Through an approach to education, which is not based on religious belief, but simply on scientific finding, common experience, and common sense, we will find that a more compassionate mind is of immense help to maintaining a more balanced physical body. It is also necessary, in order for us to get along and to stop killing one another.

In today's reality, the well-being of over 7.5 billion human beings is very interconnected. When I first came to India as a refugee, there were six billion human beings on the planet. Some experts say that, by end of this century, the human population may reach ten billion. On top of this, a huge gap still remains between rich and poor, and global warming is becoming very crucial. The time has come to not have a sense of competition, but to harmoniously work together and share with each other—to have compassion. This is what we need for our own survival.

If people consider power to be more important than care, then human beings will continue to kill other human beings, which is untenable. If anyone feels that the present world situation, where killing a few hundred here and a few thousand there is acceptable, then the 21st century will be a miserable century with a lot of killing, suffering, and disaster. If you feel that the present situation is not right and make an effort to change it, then you are acting with compassion. Each of us has the ability to contribute to a better world. Our goal should be to create a more compassionate 21st century through education.

One day, maybe an expert will use technology to make the human brain more compassionate. Perhaps then, people will say, "Anger and attachment will always arise, so maybe it would be worthwhile to simply remove the portion of the brain connected to them." Then, there will be human beings without any feelings—that does not do a lot of good. It would be much better for us to use our sophisticated brains, to investigate, use reason, and to learn that too much anger will destroy our inner peace. To explain this, I often tell this story: "A lady with a beautiful face may be very beautiful, but when her face becomes angry, her beauty diminishes. On the other hand, if a lady who does not necessarily have a beautiful face is smiling and showing affection, she is really beautiful, isn't she?" It is helpful to see that a compassionate mind brings inner peace, and an affectionate face brings trust and conviction and forms the basis for friendship.

Notes

1. B. S. Hewlett and M. Lamb, eds., *Hunter-Gatherer Childhoods* (New Brunswick: Transactions, 2005); C. Meehan and A. Crittenden, eds., *Childhood: Origins, Evolution*

and Implications (Albuquerque: School of Advanced Research and University of New Mexico Press, 2016).

2. S. B. Hrdy, *Mothers and Others: The Evolutionary Origins of Mutual Understanding* (Cambridge, MA: Harvard University Press, 2009).

3. H. K. Kaplan; K. Hill, J. Lancaster, and A. M. Hurtado, "A Theory of Human Life History Evolution: Diet, Intelligence and Longevity," *Evolutionary Anthropology* 9, no. 4 (2000): 156–185.

4. S. B. Hrdy, *Mother Nature* (New York: Pantheon, 1999).

5. C. Kuzawa et al., "Metabolic Costs and Evolutionary Implications of Human Brain Development," *Proceedings of the National Academy of Sciences* 111, no. 36 (2014): 13010–13015.

6. K. Hawkes, J. F. O'Connell, N. G. Blurton Jones, H. Alvarez, and E. L. Charnov, "Grandmothering, Menopause, and the Evolution of Human Life Histories," *Proceedings of the National Academy of Sciences* 95, no. 3 (1998): 1336–1339.

7. K. Bard, "Emotional Engagements: How Chimpanzee Minds Develop," in *The Primate Mind*, ed. F. de Waal and P. Francesco Ferrari (Cambridge, MA: Harvard University Press, 2012), 224–225.

8. Hrdy, *Mothers and Others*, 122–124.

9. J. Perner, T. Ruffman, and S. R. Leekam, "Theory of Mind Is Contagious: You Catch It from Your Sibs," *Child Development* 65, no. 4 (1994): 1228–1235.

10. *Attachment figure* is a notion formulated by British psychiatrist and psychoanalyst John Bowlby. It refers to the person towards whom an infant is directing his/her attachment behaviors. Besides the mother who is the primary figure, there can be many other attachment figures from within or outside the family (aunt, uncle, siblings, grandmother, and close friends).

11. B. M. Repacholi and A. Gopnik, "Early Reasoning about Desire: Evidence from 14- and 18-Month Olds," *Developmental Psychology* 33, no. 1 (1997): 12–21.

12. L. B. Aknin, J. K. Hamlin, and E. W. Dunn, "Giving Leads to Happiness in Young Children," *PLOS One* 7, no. 6 (2012): 339211.

13. M. Van IJzendoorn, A. Sagi, and M. Lambermon, "The Multiple Caretaker Paradox: Data from Holland and Israel," in *Beyond the Parent: The Role of Other Adults in Children's Lives*, ed. R. C. Pianta (San Francisco: Jossey-Bass, 1992), 5–24.

14. Hrdy, *Mothers and Others*.

15. M. Kringelbach et al., "A Specific and Rapid Neural Signature for Parental Instinct," *PLOS One* 3, no. 2 (2008): e1664.

16. M. L. Glocker et al., "Baby Schema Modulates the Reward System in Nulliparous Women," *Proceedings of the National Academy of Sciences* 106, no. 22 (2009): 9115–9119.

17. E. Abraham, T. Hendler, I. Shapira-Lichter, Y. Kanat-Maymon, O. Zagoory-Sharon, and R. Feldman, "Father's Brain Is Sensitive to Childcare Experiences," *Proceedings of the National Academy of Sciences* 111, no. 27 (2014): 9792–9797.

3 We Depend on a Harmonious Planet to Support Humanity

Johan Rockström

Your Holiness, your call for a compassionate century for the collective application of power and care for planet Earth has very strong scientific support. I would like to give you the updated scientific message of why I and members of the scientific community around the world are getting increasingly nervous about our inability to apply power and care for our future on planet Earth.

From a Small World on a Large Planet, to a Large World on a Small Planet

We have built our societies and economy on the wrong assumption: that we are a small world on a big planet. We have developed based on the belief that the oceans have unlimited stocks of fish, that forests can be cut down and greenhouse gases emitted in a planet that can absorb any kind of abuse, is always forgiving, and will not send any invoices back to humanity.

However, science clearly shows, with overwhelming evidence, that we have now tipped over to a point where, today, we are a big world on a small planet.[1] We have filled up the entire biophysical space of the planet's capacity to support humanity in the future. We are actually hitting the ceiling, where we can no longer exclude major, potentially irreversible, and catastrophic impacts that could undermine our ability in the future. I would now like to share with you three scientific insights that support this view.

Welcome to the Anthropocene

The first insight is that science welcomes the age of the Anthropocene: *Anthropos*—for us, humans—in that we, more than 7 billion people, now constitute the largest geological force of change on planet Earth. We are such a large force that, today, we have even started the sixth mass extinction

Earth system trends

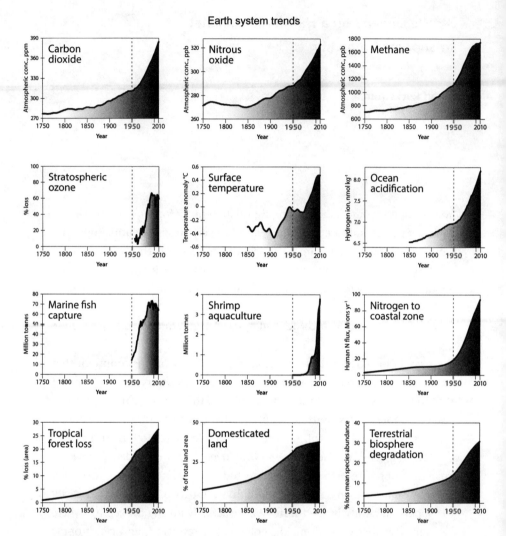

Figure 3.1
The great acceleration of pressures on our planet.
Source: Azote image for Stockholm Resilience Centre

Socio-economic trends

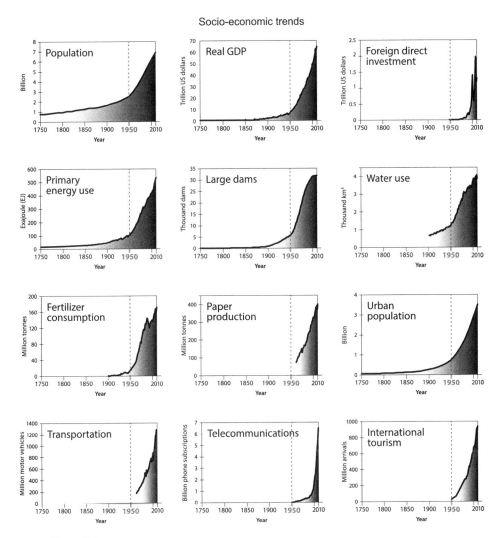

Figure 3.1
(continued)

of species on planet Earth; the first caused by another species. This is not built on assumptions, but on observations.

The Great Acceleration of Pressures on Our Planet

The graph in figure 3.1 shows the enormous evidence we have on what has happened on our planet, starting from the Industrial Revolution in 1750 in the United Kingdom until today.

What we see on the x-axis is a pattern of very gradual impact on planet Earth, which then suddenly kicks off into an exponential rise. Normally, we focus only on one of these trends, which is carbon dioxide. Yet, if you take any parameter on this chart that relates to humans—from forests, to fish, to air quality, to the one that makes me most nervous, which is the exponential rise in our killing off other animals and plants on planet Earth—all of these display an enormous increase of pressures on the planet.

Scientifically, we see increasing evidence that planet Earth had the resilience to fully absorb this pressure up until roughly 1990. Before that, we have no evidence of abrupt consequences from interactions at local and global scales from increasing greenhouse gases, deforestation, or overfishing. But, starting 25 to 30 years ago, we begin to observe and document abrupt and significant shifts: the collapse of the Atlantic Northwest cod fisheries, an acceleration in the melting of Arctic sea ice, multiple collapses of freshwater ecosystems in North America and in other places including the Baltic Sea. We also see a very rapid rise in droughts and floods, and we pass 350 parts per million in CO_2 concentration, which is increasingly understood as a threshold between stability and rising instability in ice sheets, oceans, and land ecosystems.

We are concluding today that we have not only entered a whole new geological epoch, the Anthropocene, where we are in the driving seat, but that we are also responsible for the stewardship of creation on our miraculous planet, and that we face some very big risks on this journey.

The Golden Age for Humanity

The second insight is that we can now scientifically identify the Golden Age for Humanity. We can now tell what our desired state of planet Earth is, based on ice-core paleoclimatic data from glaciologists from around the world (see figure 3.2).

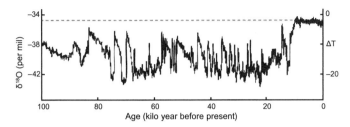

Figure 3.2
The last 100,000 years on planet Earth.
Source: Azote image for Stockholm Resilience Centre

On this graph, the x-axis represents the last 100,000 years on planet Earth. It is a wonderful period to choose because we were modern *Homo sapiens* during this entire period. We were hunter-gatherers, yet we were intellectually and physically the same as today.

On the y-axis is temperature variability, which is a good proxy of how it was to live on Earth during this time. The temperature in the Ice Age was jumpy. In fact, over ten years, it could rise and go down by ten degrees Celsius. There was a point, roughly 75,000 years ago, where it was so cold that fresh water was tied up in the polar regions, sea levels were over a hundred meters lower, and genetic paleoclimatic data show that there were fewer than 15,000 fertile adult *Homo sapiens* left on planet Earth. Our ancestors were hiding in the Ethiopian highlands—the only place where there was water and food to be found—and we were virtually extinct. This tells us how dependent we are on a stable planet; it also shows that we are all very close relatives. Roughly 10,000 years ago, something changed, which is seen in the circle (figure 3.3). This is the start of the Golden Age, or the Holocene epoch.

Now, we barely enter the Holocene and we make the most crucial transition of all during the entire history of humanity on Earth: we go from being hunter-gatherers to being farmers. We invent agriculture, and we know today that this was not a eureka moment, where the farmers suddenly said, "Oh my God, what a beautiful idea! Let me plant a seed." No. It all happened at the same moment with rice in Asia, maize in Latin America, and with teff in Ethiopia, thanks to the fact that the planet settled in and became more harmonious.[2] The rainy seasons became predictable. Farmers knew every year they could plant, grow, and harvest.

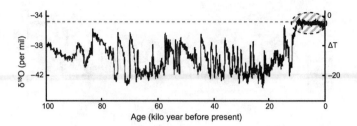

Figure 3.3
Showcasing the jumpy period of the last 100,000 years, and the start of the Golden Age of the Holocene period 10,000 years ago.
Source: Azote image for Stockholm Resilience Centre

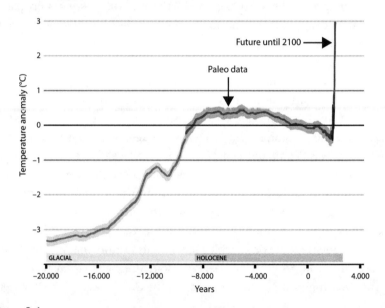

Figure 3.4
We depend on a harmonious planet for our survival.
Source: Azote image for Stockholm Resilience Centre

This change was so fantastic that the latest climatic data show something remarkable. On the x-axis in figure 3.4, you see the last 20,000 years. On the y-axis, you see the temperature on Earth. You see minus three degrees Celsius in the deep Ice Age, and then an exit into this miraculous Holocene epoch between plus/minus one degree Celsius.

This is the dramatic conclusion of science today: that we depend on a harmonious planet within this Holocene period to support humanity.

Hitting the Ceiling to Support Humanity

Now, our planet is hitting the ceiling. We have warmed one degree Celsius, and we are reaching far out of this level. If you take data from the last 2,000 years, look at where we are heading (figure 3.5). Even if we would adopt and implement what we have today as promises in the Paris Agreement on Climate Change, we would actually go up to three degrees Celsius, a place we have not even been in the last five million years. So, we are playing a very dramatic game with planet Earth.

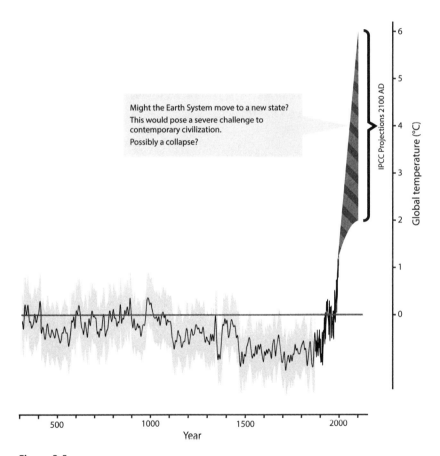

Figure 3.5
Projections show that we are moving towards three degrees Celsius. IPCC, Intergovernmental Panel on Climate Change.
Source: Azote image for Stockholm Resilience Centre

Everything We Cherish Has Settled into the Holocene

Everything we love and we care for settles in the Holocene: the coral reefs, which support 250 million coastal communities around the world; the temperate forests, which serve as massive carbon sinks on planet Earth; the rainforests; the ice sheets that reflect incoming heat back to space and keep us safe; and the freshwater systems in the Iguaçú Falls. The second insight is that we depend on the Holocene for our future.[3]

Facing Potentially Catastrophic Tipping Points

The third and final insight is that we cannot exclude catastrophic tipping points. We abuse planet Earth. How will she respond? We have major evidence today that planet Earth does not respond in a linear way, but rather in an abrupt and surprising way. The latest data shows our exit from the last Ice Age and entrance into the Holocene (figure 3.6).

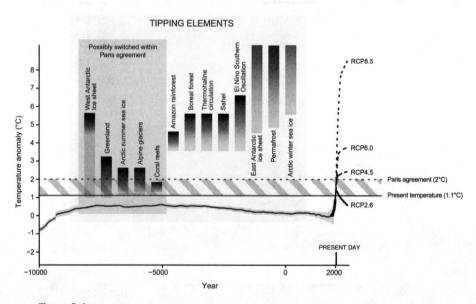

Figure 3.6
Why there is strong scientific support for staying under 2°C global warming as agreed to in Paris.
Source: Azote image for Stockholm Resilience Centre

The gray striped field is the Paris range, where we are aiming to reduce global warming to under two degrees Celsius. Yet, the coral reefs, alpine glaciers, and even the Greenland Ice Sheet are at risk of being irreversibly lost already at two degrees Celsius. This puts us at risk for abrupt tipping points. Polar land systems, like the beautiful Svalbard, need to be permanently white to reflect incoming heat to space and keep the planet cool. The coral reefs are also being permanently lost due to overfishing, nutrient pollution, and climate change.

Anthropocene + Holocene + Tipping Points = Planetary Boundaries

These three insights lead to an equation that requires a new compassion for our planet. We have entered the Anthropocene. We are now the driving force of planetary change. We are dependent on the Holocene. We need to return to a harmonious level on planet Earth. We know today that tipping points are real, and that we cannot exclude them. If we add these together, it requires us to define planetary boundaries, and the space within which we can have a good future for humanity on Earth, and science can do this today. Scientifically, we have now identified the processes that regulate the stability of the planet, and we are able to quantify the levels within which we can have a safe operating space for humanity without risk of catastrophic pushes of the whole planet out of the Holocene. If we go outside these levels, we risk dramatic change. This safe operating space gives us hope for power and care for the future (see figure 3.7).

Now, we can do a lot with this science. For instance, just 150 years ago, we know that with the advent of the Industrial Revolution, we were right in the middle of these boundaries and had the safe operating space on our side. Already in the 1950s, though, we had adopted modern agriculture and expanded rapidly. This led us to a very dangerous point on the loss of biodiversity. Today, agriculture has expanded to a point where it takes up 50% of the Earth's surface. Despite this, in the 1950s, we still remained within the safe operating space for all of the other processes that regulate the planet: climate change, water, chemicals, land, biodiversity, and forests (figure 3.8a). Through the 1960s and 1970s, we continued developing and

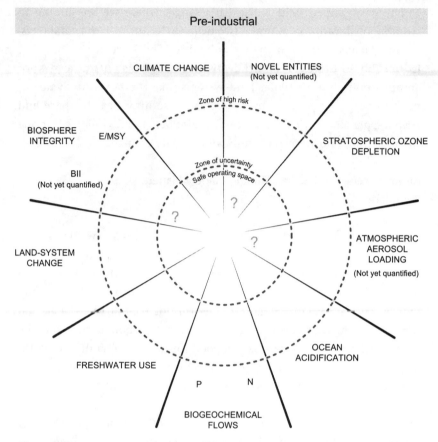

Figure 3.7
Planetary boundaries have been defined to provide a safe operating space for humanity.
Notes: E/MSY = extinction per million species per year; BII = Biodiversity Inactness Index; P = Phosphorous cycle; N = Nitrogen cycle
Source: Azote image for Stockholm Resilience Centre

remained inside the green space (figure 3.8b). Then, the big bang comes in 1990, when we transgressed the boundaries on climate change, nutrients, biodiversity, and the protective stratospheric ozone layer (figure 3.8c).

Today, we are still outside of many boundaries, but if one looks carefully, the ozone layer was in a very catastrophic danger point in 1990, but it came back in to the safe operating space (figure 3.8d). Why? Because humanity listened to science, and nations signed and implemented the

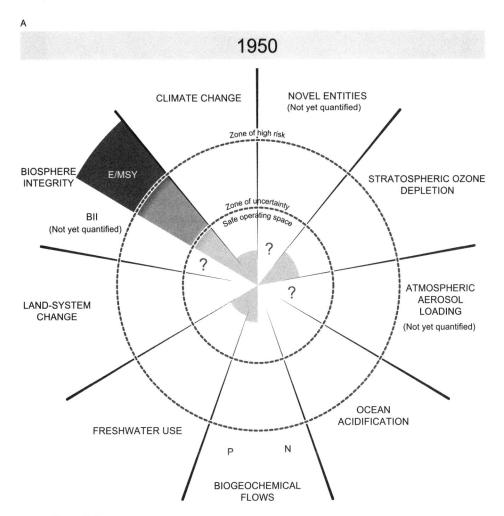

Figure 3.8
Planetary boundaries from the Industrial Revolution until today.
Source: Azote image for Stockholm Resilience Centre

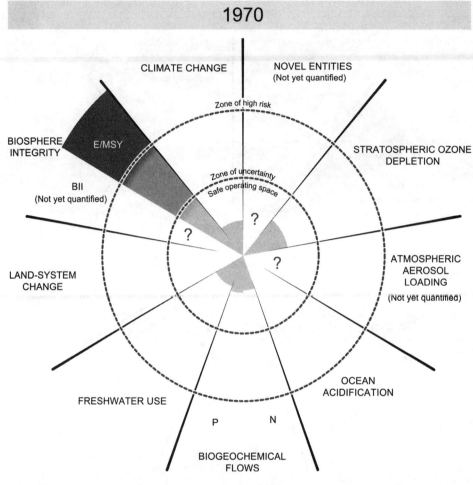

Figure 3.8
(continued)

C

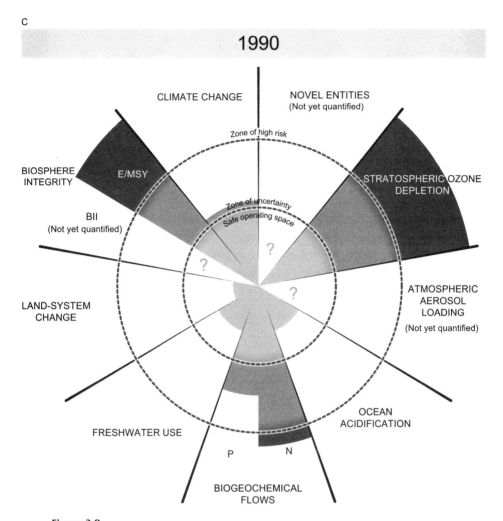

Figure 3.8
(continued)

42 Johan Rockström

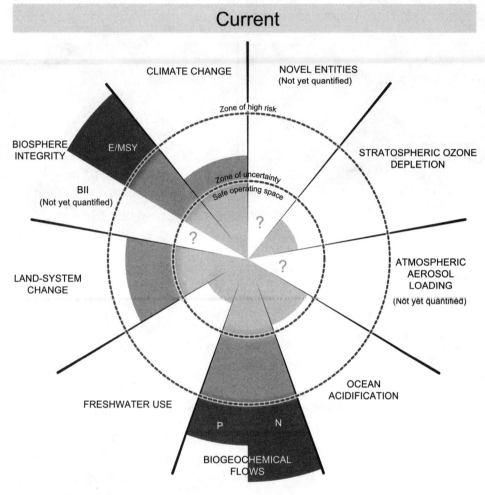

Figure 3.8
(continued)

Montreal Protocol, to collectively apply power and care. As a result, our planet avoided a disaster for humanity: the destruction of the stratospheric ozone layer that protects us from dangerous ultraviolet radiation, which could actually kill off large parts of species on Earth. This is a promising story for humanity.

Delivering a Better, More Harmonious Future for Humanity

In closing, what does all this imply for our future? The Paris Agreement shows that we need to transform within the next 30 to 40 years into a fossil-fuel-free civilization. It will be a dramatic transformation—which has all to do with power and care—and the beauty is that we have so much evidence that we can deliver a better, more harmonious future for humanity.

The United Nations has adopted the 17 Sustainable Development Goals—aspirational goals to eradicate poverty and hunger and create a harmonious future within the boundaries we have defined for our climate, water, biodiversity, and oceans (figure 3.9a). My suggestion is that we take on these goals, but that we think of them as a harmonious, caring, wedding cake for humanity and the future, where the biosphere is nonnegotiable, so that we stay within the safe operating space of our planetary boundaries (figure 3.9b).

We want to have aspirational social goals and to use economic development to achieve them, but let us once and for all transition in power and care for planet Earth, not for protecting nature, but for protecting humanity in the future.

The Dalai Lama: Wonderful. Thank you. This is a presentation that gives us hope. (Laughter.)

There is a real basis for a bright future, but it requires us to act accordingly and to make an effort. We may find this temporarily uncomfortable or difficult, but with long-term vision and self-confidence, we can train our brain to provide infinite love and compassion. If we combine these two things, after millions of years, who knows what is possible.

I am a monk. I do not have children or grandchildren, but by taking action, we can feel comfortable for the next few centuries and make the world a safe and healthy place. The scientific research is giving us a clear picture of reality from multiple dimensions. Just seeing what is reality cannot change our wish, so we have to take action.

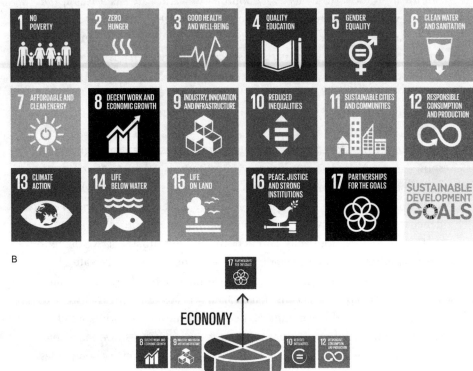

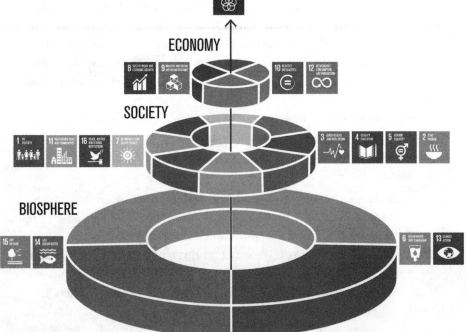

Figure 3.9
Redrawing the Sustainable Development Goals to ensure we stay within a safe operating space of planetary boundaries.
Source: Azote image for Stockholm Resilience Centre

Notes

1. Johan Rockström, and Mattias Klum, *Big World, Small Planet: Abundance within Planetary Boundaries* (New Haven, CT: Yale University Press, 2015) [in English].

2. Teff is a grain that is the staple food of Ethiopian people and inhabitants of other countries of the Horn of Africa, where it is cultivated.

3. The Iguaçú Falls are located in the middle of a tropical rainforest between Argentina and Brazil. They are described on the UNESCO World Heritage site.

II   Perspectives from Psychology, Endocrinology, and Neuroscience

This second session moves away from the big picture, to explore what happens inside the experience of the human being at the level of psychology, endocrinology, and neuroscience. With this, the psychological considerations of power and care in relation to the power motive are presented by Alexandra Freund. Markus Heinrichs provides his research on social hormones in the human brain, and emerging data from The ReSource Project, which focuses on the effect of meditation and mental training practices, is presented by Tania Singer. Lastly, Richard Schwartz offers ways to transform one's shadows through mindful awareness to balance power and care for a brighter future.

—Roshi Joan Halifax, Ph.D., second-session moderator, a Buddhist teacher, anthropologist, and abbot at the Upaya Zen Center in Santa Fe, New Mexico, USA

4   Psychological Considerations of the Power Motive

Alexandra M. Freund

When you think about a power-motivated individual, who comes to mind? Often, one thinks of Hitler, or Stalin, or Mao Zedong—individuals whose power motives have had extremely negative and devastating consequences for humankind. However, now think of Mahatma Gandhi. While he may be considered as one of the most caring people, Gandhi was also highly power motivated. He took the power away from the British by leading the Indian people into a peaceful fight for independence—and one needs power to do this. Today, I will use research in psychology to look at both sides of the power motive: the negative side, which comes to mind more easily, and the positive, caring aspects of power, which can help to create a better world.

What Is a Power Motive?

Power motive is a term that is often used in psychology. First, it is important to point out that a "motive" is not the same as "motivation." Motivation is the fuel that enables you to take action, or direct your thoughts, while a motive is the goal toward which you direct your fuel. It defines the direction of your actions or thoughts. A power motive is defined as the motive to exert influence and control over the environment and other people. This means that a motive-driven person wants to change the environment, including other people, according to his or her goals.

Some psychologists claim that a power motive is central to our development, as everyone exerts a certain amount of control within his or her environment, just like one could argue that Mahatma Gandhi shaped the Indian environment to lead the Indian people to independence.

Power, in itself, can be a relatively stable disposition, or it can be a momentary state. Research has shown that the degree of one's personal power motive or power disposition is very stable throughout an entire life span, but what can change dramatically from one moment to the next is the power motive state—the moment in time when one is triggered and decides to exert power.

How to Assess One's Power Motive

Researchers use questionnaires to assess the conscious and unconscious aspects of the power motive via a self-report.[1] Participants are asked to respond to statements including "I like to have the final say," by answering to what degree this statement applies. Responses are then aggregated into a global score, indicating the degree to which people are power-motivated. Studies have shown that these scores are associated with power-related behaviors and cognitions.

There are also ways to tap into the more subconscious aspects of the power motive.[2] For example, an exercise can include giving a participant an image that shows the captain of a ship talking to a man wearing a hat. We would ask participants, "What is going on here?" As a next step, we would code the participant's stories according to how much power motive is being expressed. If the participant said, "Well, the captain is clearly the boss. He is explaining to the passenger how the voyage will go," I can determine that the power motive is fairly high: the boss is superior and the passenger is subordinate. However, if a participant said, "The two have just met; they are looking forward to their dinner together, when they will have more time to talk," then, clearly, this response is not very power motivated.

Social Consequences of Power

There are also procedures that enable researchers to activate the state of power, which is highly malleable from moment to moment. In the laboratory, participants are asked to think about low-power conditions—situations when others had power over them. Alternatively, they are asked to think of situations where they were put into higher conditions of power. Another way to activate someone's power state is to assign a role. Surprisingly, simply telling somebody in an experiment, "You're the boss," and telling another, "You're not," has significant consequences for how powerful people feel.

What happens when we experimentally manipulate people to feel in power, or if they are dispositionally power motivated? There are strong social consequences. Overall, people in positions of power pay less attention to what is going on with others—how they feel, what they might want—which has a lot of negative effects.[3] In addition, the level of compassion for the suffering of others decreases.[4] This is important, as this also holds true outside of an experimental setting, affecting the level of compassion in a partnership. The power motive can influence relationships not only with groups, but also with individuals who are close to the person. It increases the objectification of others, and the use of others as a means, by calculating, "Does this person help me to achieve my goals or not?"[5] This also decreases the willingness to help others, and to sacrifice one's interests on behalf of others, through donations, for instance.[6] Powerful people are more likely to say: "Other people are just the same as me. They are not trustworthy. I cannot trust their compassion, because they basically want to use me to achieve their goals." Power decreases trust and increases cynicism.[7] It also decreases the desire for interpersonal harmony.[8]

It is less obvious, but there are also positive sides of power. Powerful people pay less attention to others. As a result, empirical evidence from experiments has shown that people in positions of power feel less distressed in socially stressful situations.[9] Their resilience is also increased when they are socially excluded.[10] Furthermore, power can increase the ability to infer others' thoughts and feelings if the person is a prosocial person to begin with.[11] So, paradoxically, even though you generally pay less attention to others in a power situation, if you are a very caring person, you will be better tuned-in. Powerful people have more social ties and report having more friendships.[12] People in a position of power feel more authentic, and are perceived as being more authentic. They also report more happiness, as well as higher levels of subjective well-being.[13]

Embracing Our Power for the Benefit of Humankind

To sum up, there is a dark side of power. People in powerful positions have a higher likelihood of manipulating others and using them strategically to achieve their goals. Power can also corrupt, because of a lack of accountability and checks and balances. This leads to a perception of entitlement. Yet, there is also a bright side of power. It fosters authenticity, increases subjective well-being, and empowers people to act according to their goals. This is the side of power that future research studies should focus on because it might increase altruism and help to create future leaders like Gandhi and Martin Luther King, Jr.—men who led others but who also used their power for compassion and for caring. The goal is not to move away from the power motive but to instead embrace the power we carry in us, and in the positions we take, and use it for a more caring and compassionate world.

Notes

1. Felix D. Schönbrodt and Friederike X. R. Gerstenberg, "An IRT Analysis of Motive Questionnaires: The Unified Motive Scales," *Journal of Research in Personality* 46, no. 6 (2012): 725–742.

2. Oliver C. Schultheiss, Diana Yankova, Benjamin Dirlikov, and Daniel J. Schad, "Are Implicit and Explicit Motive Measures Statistically Independent? A Fair and Balanced Test Using the Picture Story Exercise and a Cue- and Response-Matched Questionnaire Measure," *Journal of Personality Assessment* 91, no. 1 (2011): 72–81.

3. Adam D. Galinsky, Joe C. Magee, M. Ena Inesi, and Deborah H. Gruenfeld, "Power and Perspectives Not Taken," *Psychological Science* 17, no. 12 (2006): 1068–1074.

4. Gerben A. van Kleef, Christopher Oveis, Ilmo van der Löwe, Aleksandr LuoKogan, Jennifer Goetz, and Dacher Keltner, "Power, Distress, and Compassion," *Psychological Science* 19, no. 12 (2008): 1315–1322.

5. Deborah H. Gruenfeld, M. Ena Inesi, Joe C. Magee, and Adam D. Galinsky, "Power and the Objectification of Social Targets," *Journal of Personality and Social Psychology* 95, no. 1 (2008): 111–127.

6. Joris Lammers, Adam D. Galinsky, Ernestine H. Gordijn, and Sabine Otten, "Power Increases Social Distance," *Social Psychological and Personality Science* 3, no. 3 (2012): 282–290; Francesca Righetti, Laura B. Luchies, Suzanne van Gils, Erica B. Slotter, Betty Witcher, and Madoka Kumashiro, "The Prosocial versus Proself Power Holder: How Power Influences Sacrifice in Romantic Relationships," *Personality and Social Psychology Bulletin* 41, no. 6 (2015): 779–790.

7. M. Ena Inesi, Deborah H. Gruenfeld, and Adam D. Galinsky, "How Power Corrupts Relationships: Cynical Attributions for Others' Generous Acts," *Journal of Experimental Social Psychology* 48, no. 4 (2012): 795–803.

8. Seymour Adler, "Subordinate Imitation of Supervisor Behavior: The Role of Supervisor Power and Subordinate Self-Esteem," *Social Behavior and Personality* 11, no. 2 (1983): 5–10; John T. Copeland, "Prophecies of Power: Motivational Implications of

Social Power for Behavioral Confirmation," *Journal of Personality and Social Psychology* 67, no. 2 (1994): 264–277.

9. Dana R. Carney, Amy J. C. Cuddy, and Andy J. Yap, "Review and Summary of Research on the Embodied Effects of Expansive (vs. Contractive) Nonverbal Displays," *Psychological Science* 26, no. 5 (2015): 657–663; Maya M. Kuehn, Serena Chen, and Amie M. Gordon, "Having a Thicker Skin—Social Power Buffers the Negative Effects of Social Rejection," *Social Psychological and Personality Science* 6, no. 6 (2015): 701–709; Petra C. Schmid and Marianne Schmid Mast, "Power Increases Performance in a Social Evaluation Situation as a Result of Decreased Stress Responses," *European Journal of Social Psychology* 43, no. 3 (2013): 201–211.

10. Jayanth Narayanan, Kenneth Tai, and Zoe Kinias, "Power Motivates Interpersonal Connection Following Social Exclusion," *Organizational Behavior and Human Decision Processes* 122, no. 2 (2013): 257–265.

11. Stéphane Côté, Michael W. Kraus, Bonnie Hayden Cheng, Christopher Oveis, Ilmo van der Löwe, Hua Lian, and Dacher Keltner, "Social Power Facilitates the Effect of Prosocial Orientation on Empathic Accuracy," *Journal of Personality and Social Psychology* 101, no. 2 (2011): 217–232; Marianne Schmid Mast, Klaus Jonas, and Judith A. Hall, "Give a Person Power and He or She Will Show Interpersonal Sensitivity: The Phenomenon and Its Why and When," *Journal of Personality and Social Psychology* 97, no. 5 (2009): 835–850.

12. Richard S. Blackburn, "Lower Participant Power: Toward a Conceptual Integration," *The Academy of Management Review* 6, no. 1 (1981): 127–131; Herminia Ibarra, "Race, Opportunity, and Diversity of Social Circles in Managerial Networks," *Academy of Management Journal* 38, no. 3 (1995): 673–703.

13. Adam Waytz, Eileen Y. Chou, Joe C. Magee, and Adam D. Galinsky, "Not So Lonely at the Top: The Relationship between Power and Loneliness," *Organizational Behavior and Human Decision Processes* 130 (September 2015): 69–78; Yona Kifer, Daniel Heller, Wei Qi Elaine Perunovic, and Adam D. Galinsky, "The Good Life of the Powerful: The Experience of Power and Authenticity Enhances Subjective Well-being," *Psychological Science* 24, no. 3 (2013): 280–288.

5 The Biology of Care: Social Hormones in the Human Brain

Markus Heinrichs

Your Holiness, I would like to talk about the biology of care and, more specifically, about how the hormone oxytocin influences human social behavior in the brain.

The Breastfeeding Hormone Oxytocin and the Chemistry of Care

We have known for nearly 100 years that birth and breastfeeding are regulated by oxytocin. When a baby initiates the suckling stimulus, this ancient hormone, oxytocin, is released from the human brain into the bloodstream, entering the breast and making milk ejection possible.[1] Apart from breastfeeding, oxytocin has also become one of the most prominent molecules to be studied in the last decade for its role in building social attachment, care, and trust.[2]

Over the past 15 years, we have demonstrated that oxytocin is not only produced in the brain, but also distributed to those brain regions that are important for social behavior and emotional processing.[3] Studies on animal behavior have shown that oxytocin has an effect on regulating maternal behavior, social attachment, and pair bonding, and that it also provides better control in stressful social situations.[4] More recent work in humans has exhibited similar results: oxytocin improves social-emotional abilities and enables individuals to maintain eye contact, which is an important factor in establishing care and trust, maternal behavior, and pair bonding.[5] Our studies have also confirmed that oxytocin gives individuals better control over their stress response in socially threatening situations.

The Role of Oxytocin in Regulating Stress

To understand the role of oxytocin in regulating our stress reactivity, we use a laboratory setting called the Trier Social Stress Test.[6] This test is widely used by human researchers around the world and consists of a five-minute public speaking task in front of a critical panel of evaluators, resembling an interview when applying for a job; followed by five minutes of mental arithmetic during which the person has to count backward from 2,023 in 17 steps. This procedure leads to dramatic increases in the stress hormone cortisol, blood pressure, and psychological stress responses.

What is striking in stress research is the difference between men and women with regard to the stress-buffering effect of social support. Using the stress test, we demonstrated that the social support a man provides and that a woman provides differ considerably.[7] When men come alone to the stress test, they exhibit a significant stress response. If men are supported by a woman they have never met before, their stress response drops slightly. But if the men are allowed to bring their own wives or partners, it proves to be most beneficial regarding their stress response. For women, we observe an entirely different story: women, on average, exhibit lower stress levels than men when they arrive alone to the stress test. Studies reveal that they do not benefit from support coming from a man they have never met before. However, when women are asked to bring their own husbands or partners to this stress test, their level of stress actually rises strongly (see figure 5.1).

The scientific evidence indicates that positive physical contact can be much more powerful than speaking when it comes to reducing stress in humans. I would like to share two experiments that illustrate this. One experiment stimulates the oxytocin system through physical contact: a neck/shoulder massage. In the second experiment, oxytocin is administered via nasal spray to the brain to measure what happens in the context of stress and social support. In the physical contact study,[8] we found the following: in comparison to the stress response of women who come alone to the stress test showing a normal response in the stress hormone cortisol, the stress response of women who were supported verbally by their husbands or partners was again higher. But if men were not allowed to speak and were only instructed to apply a neck/shoulder massage before stress, women showed a dramatically reduced stress response for about one hour. These results demonstrate that the power of touch is highly protective against stress (see figure 5.2).

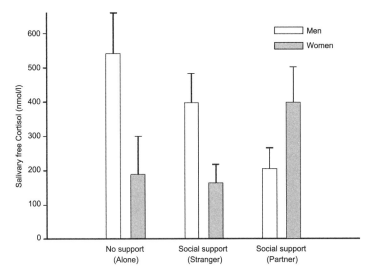

Figure 5.1
Social support's effect on reducing stress differs considerably between men and women.
Source: Figure modified, with permission, from C. Kirschbaum, T. Klauer, S. H. Filipp, and D. H. Hellhammer, "Sex-Specific Effects of Social Support on Cortisol and Subjective Responses to Acute Psychological Stress," *Psychosomatic Medicine*, 57, no. 1 (1995): 23–31.

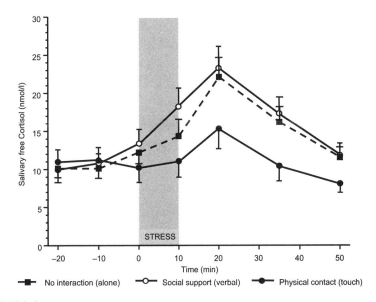

Figure 5.2
Physical contact but not verbal support provided by male partners induced the greatest reduction in stress for women.
Source: Figure modified, with permission, from B. Ditzen, I. D. Neumann, G. Bodenmann, B. von Dawans, R. A. Turner, U. Ehlert, and M. Heinrichs, "Effects of Different Kinds of Couple Interaction on Cortisol and Heart Rate Responses to Stress in Women," *Psychoneuroendocrinology*, 32, no. 5 (2007): 565–574.

In the first study in humans using oxytocin in the social context, we administered oxytocin or a placebo via nasal spray, and the subjects received social support or no support before the stress test.[9] This revealed two extreme responses: the men who received no social support and a placebo revealed the highest stress response overall while those who received both protective factors—higher oxytocin levels in the brain *and* social support—showed the lowest social stress response (see figure 5.3).

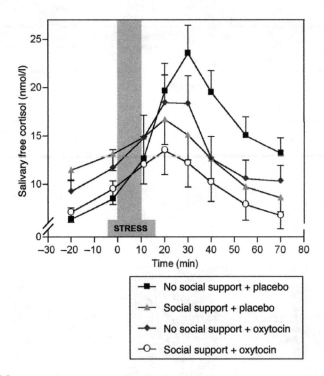

Figure 5.3
Men who received no social support or oxytocin exhibited the highest stress responses, and those receiving social support and oxytocin had the lowest stress responses.
Source: Figure modified, with permission, from M. Heinrichs, T. Baumgartner, C. Kirschbaum, and U. Ehlert, "Social Support and Oxytocin Interact to Suppress Cortisol and Subjective Responses to Psychosocial Stress," *Biological Psychiatry*, 54, no. 12 (2003): 1389–1398.

Oxytocin and Empathy, Care, and Attachment

Finally, I would also like to mention eye contact as an important prerequisite for the development of empathy, care, and attachment. Eye contact starts in the very first days of life, with mom, dad, a sister, or a brother, and plays a major role in one's social interactions throughout life. With the Reading the Mind in the Eyes Test,[10] which was developed for autism, the ability of "reading" emotions from another individual's eyes can be measured. Test participants are asked to say, from looking at the depicted eye region of a person, what that person is feeling or thinking. What we observe with this study is that higher levels of oxytocin in the brain following intranasal administration improves the ability to read emotions in another's eye region both in healthy individuals[11] and in those with autism[12] (see figure 5.4).

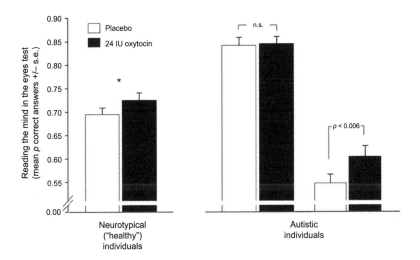

Figure 5.4

Oxytocin enables both healthy and autistic individuals to read emotions in the eye region of others more accurately.

Notes: * and *p* value represent statistically significant differences; n.s. means no significant difference.

Source: Figures modified, with permission, from G. Domes, M. Heinrichs, A. Michel, C. Berger, and S. C. Herpertz, "Oxytocin Improves 'Mind-Reading' in Humans" (Priority Communication), *Biological Psychiatry* 61, no. 6 (2007): 731–733; and A. J. Guastella, S. L. Einfeld, K. M. Gray, N. J. Rinehart, B. J. Tonge, T. J. Lambert, and I. B. Hickie, "Intranasal Oxytocin Improves Emotion Recognition for Youth with Autism Spectrum Disorders," *Biological Psychiatry*, 67, no. 7 (2010): 692–694.

Oxytocin is not just relevant for individual behavior in social situations. It may also represent a biological basis for the intergenerational transmission of care and attachment in humans.[13] For instance, parents who have a better functioning oxytocin system are likely to respond more empathically to their baby's cry and may control stress better when infants are crying. This results in more responsive, affectionate caregiving. Because this empathic response may stimulate the baby's oxytocin system, these babies are more likely to become more securely attached children and adults. This level of empathy will also be transferred to the next generation when those adults go on to become parents themselves. Thus, the oxytocin system may be relevant as a biological mechanism to transfer attachment and caregiving from one generation to the next.

To summarize, to understand care, as seen from the mind–body dialogue perspective, we need to consider the neurobiological basis of caregiving and of social interaction,[14] in particular when it comes to developing future treatment strategies for individuals with severe social deficits.[15]

Notes

1. M. Heinrichs and G. Domes, "Neuropeptides and Social Behavior: Effects of Oxytocin and Vasopressin in Humans," *Progress in Brain Research* 170 (December 2008): 337–350.

2. B. Ditzen and M. Heinrichs, "Psychobiology of Social Support: The Social Dimension of Stress Buffering," *Restorative Neurology and Neuroscience* 32, no. 1 (2014): 149–162; M. Kosfeld,* M. Heinrichs,* P. Zak, U. Fischbacher, and E. Fehr, "Oxytocin Increases Trust in Humans," *Nature* 435, no. 7042 (2005): 673–676 (*shared first authorship).

3. M. Heinrichs, B. von Dawans, and G. Domes, "Oxytocin, Vasopressin, and Human Social Behavior," *Frontiers in Neuroendocrinology* 30, no. 4 (2009): 548–557.

4. Z. R. Donaldson and L. J. Young, "Oxytocin, Vasopressin, and the Neurogenetics of Sociality," *Science* 322, no. 5903 (2008): 900–904.

5. A. Meyer-Lindenberg, G. Domes, P. Kirsch, and M. Heinrichs, "Oxytocin and Vasopressin in the Human Brain: Social Neuropeptides for Translational Medicine," *Nature Reviews Neuroscience* 12, no. 9 (2011): 524–538.

6. B. von Dawans, C. Kirschbaum, and M. Heinrichs, "The Trier Social Stress Test for Groups (TSST-G): A New Research Tool for Controlled Simultaneous Social Stress Exposure in a Group Format," *Psychoneuroendocrinology* 36, no. 4 (2011): 514–522.

7. C. Kirschbaum, T. Klauer, S. H. Filipp, and D. H. Hellhammer, "Sex-Specific Effects of Social Support on Cortisol and Subjective Responses to Acute Psychological Stress," *Psychosomatic Medicine* 57, no. 1 (1995): 23–31.

8. B. Ditzen, I. D. Neumann, G. Bodenmann, B. von Dawans, R. A. Turner, U. Ehlert, and M. Heinrichs, "Effects of Different Kinds of Couple Interaction on Cortisol and Heart Rate Responses to Stress in Women," *Psychoneuroendocrinology* 32, no. 5 (2007): 565–574.

9. M. Heinrichs, T. Baumgartner, C. Kirschbaum, and U. Ehlert, "Social Support and Oxytocin Interact to Suppress Cortisol and Subjective Responses to Psychosocial Stress," *Biological Psychiatry* 54, no. 12 (2003): 1389–1398.

10. S. Baron-Cohen, S. Wheelwright, J. Hill, Y. Raste, and I. Plumb, "The 'Reading the Mind in the Eyes' Test, Revised Version: A Study with Normal Adults, and Adults with Asperger Syndrome or High-Functioning Autism," *Journal of Child Psychology and Psychiatry* 42, no. 2 (2001): 241–251.

11. G. Domes, M. Heinrichs, A. Michel, C. Berger, and S. C. Herpertz, "Oxytocin Improves 'Mind-Reading' in Humans" (Priority Communication), *Biological Psychiatry* 61, no. 6 (2007): 731–733.

12. A. J. Guastella, S. L. Einfeld, K. M. Gray, N. J. Rinehart, B. J. Tonge, T. J. Lambert, and I. B. Hickie, "Intranasal Oxytocin Improves Emotion Recognition for Youth with Autism Spectrum Disorders," *Biological Psychiatry* 67, no. 7 (2010): 692–694.

13. J. K. Rilling and L. J. Young, "The Biology of Mammalian Parenting and Its Effect on Offspring Social Development," *Science* 345, no. 6198 (2014): 771–776.

14. M. Heinrichs, F. S. Chen, and G. Domes, "Social Neuropeptides in the Human Brain: Oxytocin and Social Behavior," in *Understanding Other Minds* (3rd ed.), ed. S. Baron-Cohen, H. Tager-Flusberg, and M. Lombardo (Oxford: Oxford University Press, 2013), 291–307.

15. M. Heinrichs, F. S. Chen, and G. Domes, "Oxytocin," in *Psychobiological Approaches for Anxiety Disorders: Treatment Combination Strategies*, ed. S. G. Hofmann (Oxford: Wiley-Blackwell, 2012), 123–143.

6 Perspectives from Contemplative Neuroscience on Power and Care: How to Train Care and Compassion

Tania Singer

Your Holiness, it is a pleasure for me to share new data on plasticity—the concept of trainability, flexibility, change, and malleability that occurs not only in our brain, but also with regard to our behavior, hormones, and stress system at all levels.

I would like to introduce you to research from The ReSource Project—a one-year-long longitudinal mental training study, where participants were followed while learning new meditation and mental training practices.[1] Based on social neuroscience knowledge, this project brought together contemplative practices from the East with psychological practices from the West, with the aim to provide the best of both worlds. Three different types of practices were trained in three separate, three-month training modules during this study, and each training module led to different changes in behavior and the brain. I would now like to share how this study was built, and how its results can be useful to inform new models of economy and help to create a more caring society (see figure 6.1).

Design of The ReSource Project, a One-Year-Long Longitudinal Study to Increase Compassion and Human Prosociality

For The ReSource Project, more than 300 participants were divided into four study cohorts, consisting of roughly 80 members each. Over the course of a year, three of the groups were trained on secular meditation practices in three separate, three-month modules called Presence, Affect, and Perspective. These mental exercises were initially taught by a total of 17 teachers at project retreats, which were held at the beginning of a given module. Afterward, these exercises were practiced once a week in smaller groups

Figure 6.1
Image of The ReSource Project participants at a project retreat.
Photo: © 2013 Sven Döring/Agentur Focus

with two teachers and at home for 20 to 30 minutes on a daily basis with the support of a cell-phone application. It is important to note that while groups one and two completed all three mental training modules, group three only undertook one three-month-long Affect module, and the study's fourth group, the so-called "retest control" group, did not undertake any training modules whatsoever. This cohort was asked to simply live their lives over the course of one year, to see if things change simply because one is getting older or because one is being continually tested with the same paradigms every three months (see figure 6.2).

Each of the three project modules had two core practice components (see figure 6.3). The first module, Presence, focused on basic mindfulness-based attention practices. It incorporated practices such as the body scan or the breathing meditation, which are similar to those implemented in the mindfulness-based stress reduction program developed by Jon Kabat-Zinn. Participants in the Presence module learned to bring their attention back to the present moment and attend to a particular object such as the breath, parts of the body, or sounds (similar to shamatha practice). The

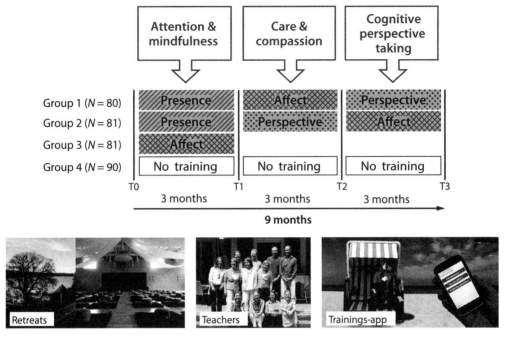

Figure 6.2
Three out of the four groups in The ReSource Project participated in three separate, three-month training modules called Presence, Affect, and Perspective over the course of nine months.
Photos: Left image © Karen Kaspar/Shotshop.com; all others ©Abteilung Soziale Neurowissenschaft

Affect module focused on cultivating care, loving-kindness, compassion, and gratitude and on dealing with and accepting difficult emotions. Participants in the Affect module practiced the loving-kindness meditation (metta meditation), as well as the Affect Dyad—a meditation done with a partner for ten minutes that was developed to cultivate these qualities.[2] The third module, Perspective, focused on taking perspective on one's own thoughts and mind, considering aspects of one's self and one's beliefs about other people. The Perspective Dyad asked participants to connect for ten minutes with another person on a daily basis and to take perspective on one's mind, on one's self, and on the mind of others by asking these questions: "What do I believe? What is the other person thinking and believing?"

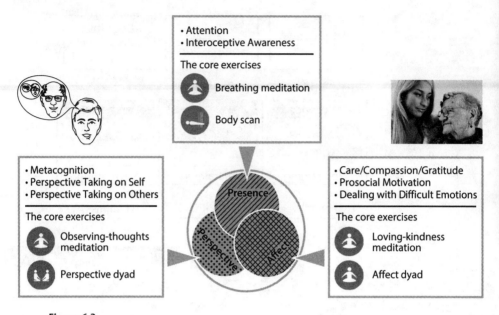

Figure 6.3
Each of the meditation practices focused on two core components.
Photo: © Lighthunter/Shotshop.com; *drawing:* © MPI-CBS, Icon © Abteilung Soziale Neurowissenschaft

The Two Different Networks of Understanding Others

His Holiness has often said that the move toward global compassion requires two wings of a bird. On one wing, it requires motivation and compassion, and on the other, intellect, wisdom, and understanding. In neuroscientific terms, this is similarly reflected in the two major and different networks or pathways for social understanding in the human brain: the emotional and the cognitive routes (see figure 6.4).

In The ReSource Project study, we measured these two different networks of socio-affective and sociocognitive understanding by putting people into a brain scanner and having them watch videos where people told stories about when they suffered in their lives. In addition to the emotional or neutral content of the stories, some stories required the participants to put themselves into the cognitive shoes of another, in order to understand his or her actions. What we observed in the brain is that if someone has a lot of compassion and empathy for the suffering of another, the network that

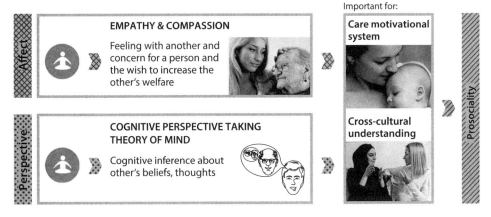

Figure 6.4
Every human brain has two major pathways for social understanding.
Photos: © Lighthunter/Shotshop.com; © petrograd99/Shotshop.com; © http://www
.photographee.eu/Shotshop.com; *drawings:* © MPI-CBS, Icon © Abteilung Soziale
Neurowissenschaft

processes social emotion is activated. This is shown in the checked pattern
in figure 6.5. In the dotted pattern, in the same brain, one can also see the
level of cognitive perspective taking on another person's mind.

These neural networks are independent of one another. This means that
some people can be good empathizers and feel the suffering with another
and yet be bad mentalizers—not very good at putting oneself in the cognitive shoes of another. It can also be the other way around. With this
information, we decided to see if we could then, by consequence, also independently cultivate these capacities through the study's Affect and Perspective modules. In the Affect module, we asked the question, "Can we train
compassion and activate the motivational, emotional care systems in the
brain and in one's behavior?" In the Perspective module, we asked, "Can we
increase the ability of people to take perspective on aspects of themselves
and others?"

Training Compassion and Care

The ReSource Project's data has shown that three months of attention-
based mindfulness practice, three months of compassion-based practice, or
three months of more cognitive perspective-taking-based exercise leads to

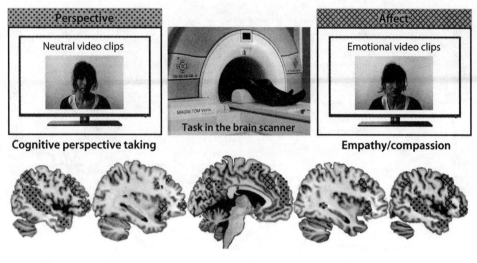

Figure 6.5
Perspective taking and empathy have distinct networks in the brain.
Sources: Scanner picture © MPI-CBS; all others © Abteilung Soziale Neurowissenschaft

a marked difference in brain plasticity, stress, and behavior. In figure 6.6, you can see that group four, the retest-control cohort that just lived their lives and grew one year older, did not become more compassionate during the course of the study. Participants who undertook three months of attention-based mindfulness exercises developed a greater ability to focus on the present moment, and the capability to augment their attention and body awareness, yet this practice did not increase their level of compassion. It was only in the care-based Affect module, where participants explicitly focused their attention and intentions on "opening the heart," by engaging in compassion, loving-kindness meditation, and gratitude practices every day, that a very specific effect was seen in boosting one's level of compassion.

Theory of Mind

Theory of Mind is the capacity to take the perspective of another's mind, that is, to understand and mentalize what other people think and believe. It is a kind of social intelligence score. The ReSource Project has shown that the practice of opening the heart will increase altruism and compassion,

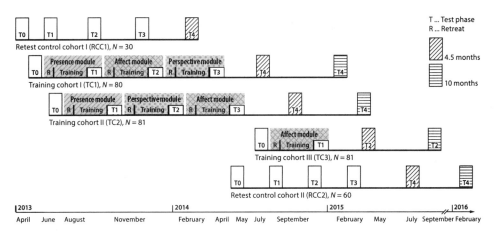

Figure 6.6
The Affect module resulted in the highest increase in compassion.

but it will not reliably enhance one's ability to understand the cognitive beliefs of others, which is a very specific effect based on the sociocognitive Perspective module. These findings additionally revealed that one can cultivate compassion and Theory of Mind through specific mental daily practices (see figure 6.7).

Structural Plasticity of the Brain: Increasing Gray Matter of the Brain through Training

The ReSource Project has revealed that daily meditation practice changes not only one's behavior, but also the very structure of one's brain. The people in this study were, on average, 43 years old. While scientists typically say that the brain declines and gray matter shrinks from age 25 onward because of aging, our tests show that we can elicit a gray-matter increase in cortical thickness in specific networks after three months of attention-based, mindfulness, socio-emotional, or cognitive mental practices. The findings revealed that both pathways of social understanding could selectively be trained. The thicker the gray matter became in an area known to be relevant for mentalizing, the better participants became in their Theory of Mind scores after Perspective training. In reverse, the thicker the insula got, the more compassion participants developed after Affect training.

Behavioral modulation of training-related cortical thickness change

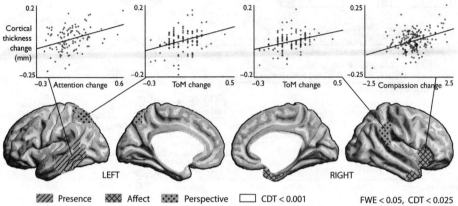

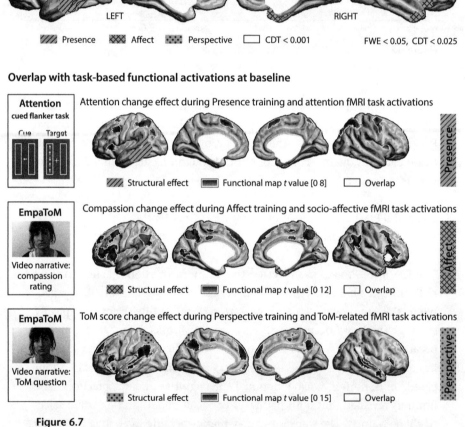

Figure 6.7
Theory of Mind (ToM) can also be cultivated through specific perspective taking training.

Notes: FWE = family-wise error [correction]; CDT = cluster-defining threshold; fMRI = functional magnetic resonance imaging.[3]

Photo: © Abteilung Soziale Neurowissenschaft

Compassion Training to Improve Prosocial Behavior and Cooperation

Other findings also showed that these compassion-based meditation practices improve prosocial behavior. In The ReSource Project, for example, we used 14 different paradigms to measure human prosociality, including psychological and also economic paradigms, where participants had to trade and give out money. From this, we could extract a factor we call pure altruism—when one gives without any expectation of reciprocation. This increased the most after the compassion-based Affect training module. This altruistic behavior thus emerged most strongly out of the quality of opening the heart.

Using The ReSource Project Data in Economics

Until now, economists have taken a classical view of economics through *Homo economicus*, the notion that human nature is selfish and simply wants to optimize its own outcomes. Yet, from The ReSource Project study, we have learned that with 20 to 30 minutes of mental training a day, a person can change from being an egoist to an altruist. This means that the classical economic view is inherently false. The so-called preferences are not fixed and stable. A more realistic picture of human nature is that we have different motivational systems, and that if we activate the care system, we will increase prosocial behavior and altruism. If we activate power, we will have competitive behavior, but sometimes also caring behavior, as Alexandra Freund previously mentioned. This information led us to conduct further experiments to see whether we could induce a power motive or induce care and then see how this plays out in economic decisions and economic behavior.

Experiments to Induce Care in the Context of Decision-Making

In order to induce care within the context of economic decision-making, we asked the test participants to watch a video about cute little puppies before playing a number of economic games where money was exchanged with other partners. To activate the care system, we explained to the participants that they would be able to engage with the pups after the game ended. To activate power motivation, we assigned power to the participants

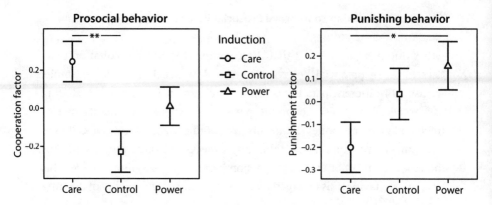

Figure 6.8
Induction of caring motivation fosters more social behavior.

by saying, "You are now the boss, and you will later have to tell a big group of people what to do." After these different motivational inductions, we measured participants' economic behavior again with multiple paradigms.

Our findings were that, after a very short care induction, one's prosocial, altruistic monetary behavior increased (see figure 6.8). By inducing power, punishment-related behavior increased and money was taken away from the other instead of being given. While such punishment-related behaviors can be useful to penalize free riders, this is a very different sort of behavior being primed than altruistic giving behaviors.

Creating Societal Change with Contemplative Practice

Our societies have important and useful methods in place to promote change through structures that include the legal system and institutional design. Yet, The ReSource Project has revealed something even more powerful: that even after the age of 25 we can increase the volume of gray matter in our brain and change our own prosocial behavior through 20 to 30 minutes of daily mental practice alone. Most of the people in The ReSource Project were working full-time and had active lives, and yet they engaged in daily short mental practices and, by consequence, the hardware of their brains—the gray-matter volume—and their behaviors were altered. This is encouraging, because if we started teaching these practices to children, who are even more plastic and malleable than adults, everyone could increase their compassion, perspective taking, and social intelligence.

Out of The ReSource Project, an institute could be developed that would serve to use mental training and education not only to shape the external world, but also to seize the power within each of us to develop ourselves inwardly. This way, we can cultivate our capacity to care, which will result in more balanced decision-making and a more compassionate society.

Notes

1. www.resource-project.org.

2. *Metta* is a Pali word, a language akin to Sanskrit, into which the Buddhist canon has been written down. In the Sutras, the word *metta* means loving-kindness, amity, good will, and benevolence.

3. The overlap with task-based functional activation at baseline refers to the fact that we had measured functional brain activation in our participants with an EmpaToM task (measuring compassion and Theory of Mind accuracy) and an attention task at baseline before the training started. We can now use these functional activation maps to see whether the peaks of the areas which show training-related increases in grey matter structure after a specific ReSource module are overlapping with these areas we observe to be functionally activated while the same participant undergoes attention, compassion, or Theory of Mind tasks. This is an adapted version of the original Eriksen Cued-Flanker Task—it measures attention both with regard to orientation to a cause and in response to inhibition. This task has been incorporated into The ReSource project to measure different aspects of human attentional capacities. Functional map t-value measures the size of the difference relative to the variation in our sample data. The greater its magnitude, the greater is the evidence against the null hypothesis that there is no significant difference.

7 Using Compassion and Mindfulness to Balance the Impulses of Power and Care

Richard Schwartz

Your Holiness, as you have been hearing from my colleagues, human systems at all levels—from countries, to families, to individuals—have two impulses: one for care and one for power. Care is the impulse to have empathy for others, to connect, open one's boundaries, and create community. The impulse of power considers the system one is in first, and how to act in the world, in order to get one's needs met and protect the boundaries of that system.

The impulses of power and care are both valuable, and the balance between them is very important. I think that Martin Luther King, Jr., and Mahatma Gandhi had access to both power and care, which is why they could act in such powerful ways. But impulses can become extreme, and when they do, they can take over and lock away the other side under certain circumstances.

When Impulses Become Extreme

Impulses can become extreme if a system has many members who are neglected, needy, and hurting. For instance, if a system has been traumatized in the past, like the chimpanzees Frans de Waal spoke about, and carries extreme emotions and beliefs from that earlier trauma, this could cause one of these impulses to become extreme and take over. Also, if a system has inherited extreme beliefs that have been passed down through the generations, or, if the system has weak or biased leadership, it can take it in one direction or the other.

Many countries are facing an immigration crisis. There are people in each country who identify with the pain of the immigrants, see them as valuable resources, and want to open the boundaries. Other people become nationalistic. They think of the country first and would like to close the boundaries. Countries, as systems, also have to find the proper balance between these impulses. If a country has a large underclass and a huge divide in income, it is going to be more vulnerable, and there will be more extremes on both sides. Also, if a country carries racist beliefs that have been passed on through the generations, then the impulse will be to go more toward power.

I have worked with families with a vulnerable child, and you will find that same power struggle in family systems. One parent identifies with the vulnerability and sensitivity of the child and wants to preserve his or her innocence and openness to the world. The other parent, however, thinks that the world will crush the child and therefore needs to make him or her tough, suspicious, and aggressive in the world. As each parent believes that the other is harming the child by what he or she is doing, each parent becomes extreme in opposing directions to the point where both are harming the child and potentially also destroying the family.

The caring side can also become extreme and cut off the power side. We did a study with 40 rheumatoid arthritis patients in Boston, Massachusetts, which was published in the *Journal of Rheumatology*.[1] Most of the patients were Irish Catholic women who had been socialized to only take care of others and not think of themselves. For the study, we simply asked the patients to focus on their pain, and instead of fighting it or trying to get away from it, to actually ask the pain questions. The patients were surprised by the answers that arose. Often, the answer came from the power side that had been exiled, saying that the pain was a way to get some kind of caring from the outside world, or that the pain was trying to sabotage the caretaking part that was so dominant. As the patients were able to create a better balance, by listening directly to the power side, their symptoms got better, and in some cases, they went into remission.

Using Mindfulness to Transform Extreme Emotions

I have also worked with people who had a dominant power side, who would carry the label "narcissistic personality" or "sociopathic personality." When working with these individuals, I ask them to do the same thing, to try and separate from that very selfish aspect of themselves by first becoming more mindful toward it, asking it what it is trying to do, and why it makes them so selfish. The answers that came back most of the time are, "If I didn't do this, I would feel powerless and worthless." As a psychotherapist, if I can get the person to focus on the worthlessness or the powerlessness, it often leads into scenes from the past where the person was made to feel that way. By opening their hearts to those memories, to those hidden aspects of themselves, the power-oriented and power-seeking aspect within them is able to shift. As a result, they can create a greater balance between power and care. I find that what are thought to be destructive emotions often are just extreme versions of one of those two motives. It is when people fight them or try to ignore them that they can become more extreme, but if I can help people to mindfully observe the destructive emotion and begin a conversation with it, they will often learn that it is really trying to protect them somehow.

Recently, I was working with a man who had a continuous impulse to kill his ex-wife. He was very frightened by this. He worked hard to distract himself from it and to lock it away. During one session, I asked him if he would be willing, instead, to try to get to know this impulse and to see if it had something to tell him. The man was resistant to this idea because he was afraid that if he would open the door to it, it would have more power, and that it might take over and make him do something he might ultimately regret. I explained to him that it really is the opposite: if he is willing to open his mind and heart to it, he will find that it can actually change. The man eventually agreed. I asked him to focus on his impulse and to ask it from a place of compassion and curiosity what it was afraid would happen if he could not kill his wife. Again, the answer came back that he would be powerless. He then saw the scene when his wife left him for another man, and how he felt so powerless. I had him focus on that feeling of powerlessness. It took him into another scene, when he was five years old, and his parents were fighting with each other. His father began to beat his mother, and his mother wound up jumping out of a window on the second floor and hurting herself. The man found that he could feel the powerlessness that boy felt. A tremendous amount of compassion overcame him and he began to cry for the boy. Once this happened, the urge to kill his wife transformed into a desire to help him find a new partner, to have that kind of power, and he was able to achieve a greater balance between power and care.

Healing Our Inner Children with Compassion

I believe that going to these vulnerable places in our histories and in our-selves releases oxytocin. I was moved by Sarah Blaffer Hrdy's image of the policemen holding babies, and if I can help very big tough men embrace these inner children this way, I believe it gives them access they previously did not have to this care.

Your Holiness, I find it very useful to go to our inner enemies with the same kind of compassion and curiosity that you advocate for us to go to our external enemies.

Note

1. Nancy A. Shadick, Nancy F. Sowell, Michelle L. Frits, Suzanne M. Hoffman, Shelley A. Hartz, Fran D. Booth, Martha Sweezy, Patricia R. Rogers, Rina L. Dubin, Joan C. Atkinson, Amy L. Friedman, Fernando Augusto, Christine K. Iannaccone, Anne H. Fossel, Gillian Quinn, Jing Cui, Elena Losina, and Richard C. Schwartz, "A Randomized Controlled Trial of an Internal Family Systems-based Psychotherapeutic Intervention on Outcomes in Rheumatoid Arthritis: A Proof-of-Concept Study," *The Journal of Rheumatology* 40, no. 11 (November 2013): 1831–1841, http://www.jrheum.org/content/40/11/1831.tab-article-info.

Dialogue with the Presenters, the Moderator, and the Dalai Lama

Roshi Joan Halifax: Your Holiness, we will now move into the dialogue part of our time together. I would like to begin by asking Alexandra, "Is there a psychological connection between power and care?"

Alexandra M. Freund: Yes. Typically, people do not see power as a very strong motive. Individuals have a tendency to shy away from power if they are not in a powerful position already. Power is seen as something that might harm others or cause us to disregard another's feelings and walk all over them. We see caring as the opposite and associate it with paying a lot of attention to what is going on in another person.

I believe that both power and care are necessary for balance. For instance, if you want to take care of somebody, you need to feel that you can actually do something that is good for the other person. It is, in a way, a power position. The other person whom we care for, however, is also not entirely powerless. He or she can refuse your care, and if you have ever been in a situation when someone refuses your care, it can be a very powerful rejection. So, it is not a simple distribution of here is power, and here is care. They are intricately intertwined. I believe, in both positions, you have aspects of one that interact very strongly with the other.

Roshi Joan Halifax: Is there a kind of third body that is the integration between power and care?

Alexandra M. Freund: I do believe that we are in dire need of a more integrated view, but at the moment, I do not know of any psychological theories or studies on the interaction between the different motive systems. We tend to look at them separately and therefore miss out on the integrated system that it is. When we act in a certain way, all of these motives come together in a specific action or according to how we perceive the world.

Richard Schwartz: I find that when I help people to observe mindfully, they can enter into a third level, or integrated state. By just getting separation from any extreme state, people can suddenly feel very calm. We have eight "C" words to describe this state: calm, curious, compassionate, connected, courageous, confident, creative, and clear. I have no idea if this can be related to some aspects of the Buddha nature described in Buddhism, but the mere act of helping people to invite these extreme aspects to open inside of them seems to release this integrated state, which seems to be a kind of essence inside of people. Once there, people have wisdom about how to create balance, and they begin to take over the sessions and actually work with each side.

Tania Singer: In neuroscience, we did research on the distinction between empathy and compassion. Empathy is defined as feeling with or getting in resonance with suffering, and the danger of this resonance is that you can turn empathy into what is called empathic distress. You find this a lot in helpers, caregivers, and doctors, who, when confronted with suffering, react with natural empathic resonance. Yet, when chronically activated, this response can subsequently turn into stress, where the person enters a pathological state and burns out. We did experiments, also as part of The ReSource Project, to teach people how to distinguish between the states of empathic resonance and compassion, and how to transform a natural empathic response into a compassionate one to prevent a move into distress.

Compassion is a very powerful, forceful, loving, and caring state, which is not to be confused with empathy in how we define it. Compassion is not feeling *with*—I am suffering, you are suffering, I am happy, you are happy—it is feeling *for*. It is feeling concern, love, and compassion for another person. As Matthieu Ricard said to me once, "You cannot burn out of compassion." It is a very powerful state of nonjudgmental acceptance. When people are able to enter into the state of compassion, their whole body posture changes, and their empathic distress vanishes. We should teach this more explicitly, especially to people in caregiving situations.

Roshi Joan Halifax: I think the word I was looking for, that integrates power and care, is compassion.

Markus Heinrichs: I would like to emphasize that things are, of course, not as easy as we have presented them. Of course, care is not only good, and power is not only bad; testosterone is not *the* power and aggression hormone, and oxytocin is not *the* love hormone. As we heard in Frans de

Waal's talk, powerful alpha male chimpanzees need to take care of the others to retain their position. When we administer testosterone to women, and then ask them to play a fairness game where they can share money or not, we observe that higher testosterone levels result in a fairer distribution of money. There is good evolutionary reason for this: if you are in a powerful position, it is beneficial to make sure that your group is happy. I therefore think it would be quite artificial to separate power and care. I find them to be interconnected in a complex manner, which makes it interesting but also difficult to find simple explanations and answers.

Roshi Joan Halifax: We now know the positive and the more negative aspects of testosterone. I think we have a biased view concerning oxytocin. Can you briefly explain its downside for us?

Markus Heinrichs: I think what's most important is to keep in mind that oxytocin, like all hormones, has no simple behavioral effect per se. If people sit at their kitchen table and administer an oxytocin nasal spray, I would predict that nothing will happen, apart from irritated nasal mucosa after chronic use. In an experimentally controlled situation, you can observe interesting and specific effects from administering hormones, but the hormone itself does not induce a complex behavior under all circumstances. In the lab, these experiments are always stimulated by a specific social situation. In therapy, oxytocin alone is, moreover, never a therapy for autism, nor for borderline personality disorder. Innovative and complex psychotherapy is required, in order to change behavior, experiences, or an attachment style. It is our hope that, by raising the level of oxytocin in the brain, we can make psychotherapy more effective in the disorders we cannot successfully treat so far—primarily in social disorders. His Holiness mentioned the interplay between culture, spirituality, and science. What we can currently offer are interesting experimental insights, mechanisms, and molecules, but these cannot explain complex human behavioral factors like compassion or care.

Roshi Joan Halifax: Tania, you have been on an extraordinary research endeavor, The ReSource Project. Could you say something about the people who were not affected by the intervention, and why you think this is the case?

Tania Singer: This is a study that took ten years of preparation and two years of testing, so we are only at the very beginning of understanding all of the complex interactions. We have different measures to analyze, from the brain, to behavior, to hormones. I have only presented changes seen at the group level because we are just starting to understand our findings. Therefore, I can only say something from observation about individual differences although we will look at this more deeply in the coming years.

What I can share is that the Presence module, which focused on mindfulness, was easy for everyone—every participant could easily accept these practices. When it came to the compassion practice, to loving-kindness through the Affect module, though, it was very obvious that in almost all three independent cohorts, there was a fraction of people who could not open their hearts so easily. They said, "I can't touch a loving, caring space in me. I can't feel this care and motivation. I don't even have an idea of a person I should imagine where I feel love." These people were blocked and had a very hard time. Some even stayed in this state for three months and were unable to do this particular practice. For others, after some weeks of practice, there came a big breakthrough with a lot of tears and crying. I cannot tell you the exact percentage of people who struggled, but I think it was about one-third, perhaps a bit less. Half were able to feel a huge amount of love, and healing occurred, while others were just blocked. We will now look at the history of these people, in terms of their attachments and anxiety levels, and identify which practice is better for whom.

Another observation we made, which has not yet been properly analyzed, was the sequence in which the modules were undertaken. One cohort did the Perspective module that focused on cognitive perspective taking first, followed by the Affect module on care and compassion, while another group completed the Affect module first, followed by the Perspective module. It seems to be easier for people to first attain a bird's-eye perspective, detachment, and equanimity before going into the "opening the heart" practices. I would like to ask His Holiness whether, in Buddhist practice, it is better to first stabilize the mind and attain basic mindful attention, before moving on to gaining perspective, and then entering into a real compassion practice, or if this is something we just discovered here, which is not matched in religious traditions?

The Dalai Lama: I appreciate people taking interest in the mind and how to deal with emotions. This is very important, as the mind is the real troublemaker. If we can work to attain peace of mind and a wider perspective, our external problems will no longer disturb us. Even our own physical pain will be manageable.

The main goal of meditation, through single-pointed concentration, or by focusing on one object, is not merely to stop a scattered mind, but to enable us to use our intelligence to cultivate compassion. At a biological level, we already have this kind of experience, but attachment hinders it on a mental level. The story about a man who was prepared to kill his ex-wife was at least partially due to a self-regarding attachment. Initially, there may have been loving-kindness and a compassionate attitude, but with time, problems arose, which led to negative feelings and grasping. What we are trying to promote is affection or compassion that is not mixed with attachment but is reached through reasoning, by valuing the pros and cons of warmheartedness versus anger and hatred. This is how we can cultivate genuine compassion that can reach even our enemy. Analytical meditation enables us to stop our harmful and negative actions in consideration of another's well-being, and develop the skills to cultivate a more positive attitude toward all beings, including our enemies, so that they will not disturb our peace of mind. This is what we call infinite love, and it only comes through training the mind.

The first level of training is the understanding that comes through hearing or reading the teachings. This provides the confidence to engage in actual meditative practice. Compassion, at this level, is something that you heard is nice. At the second level of practice, you are able to reflect upon the teachings and investigate them by using reason to bring a deep conviction. At this level, it is an effortful practice, as to familiarize this new way of being requires training and experience and can take many years. The third level is achieved through the conviction that arises as the final result of critical reflection. Due to habituation and cultivation, this level of meditation becomes an effortless state, and the experience becomes part of your nature.

To respond to Tania's question specifically, yes, there is a sequence to practicing compassion. After creating mental stability, the first step is to cultivate equanimity or a feeling that all beings deserve our love and our compassion in equal parts without bias and attachment. This means that we should not enter into reasoning that includes statements like "They are helpful for me," or "Their attitude toward me is nice." That is attachment. Similarly, having a negative attitude, hatred, anger, or suspicion must also be removed to prepare for an actual meditation on compassion.

Traditionally, two methods are used for meditating on compassion. The practice involves cultivating the attitude that all beings are your loved ones, by seeing them as having been your mothers in past lives. The other method, which is more effective, is to critically reflect upon the negative consequences of excessive self-centeredness and the positive consequences of thinking and caring more about others' well-being. For example, in *The Way of the Bodhisattva (Bodhicharyavatara)* it says, "If someone is not able to exchange one's own well-being with that of others, then not only is there no hope of attaining Buddhahood, in this life, there will not much place for happiness."[1]

No one wants to have trouble, yet many of our problems are of our own creation, due to our lack of a holistic view. If we cannot reflect on our actions, we will continue to follow a habitual, self-centered approach. This is what makes meditation helpful in teaching warmheartedness. If we say, "God says that" or "Buddha says that," someone will say, "OK, very nice," but it is our own experiences that bring true conviction. By understanding the importance of inner values, through education, humanity will be happier. This is where we need to start, not from our government or leaders, but from us as individuals. This is how society changes. First, one family becomes happier, then 10 families, 100 families, 1,000 families, and eventually an entire community, until seven billion human beings become happier.

Imbued with affection, any verbal, physical, or mental action becomes constructive. A more compassionate mind brings determination, and the healthiest form of power—a positive one—while anger brings destructive power. Everyone wants world peace, but world peace only comes through inner peace, not from anger, or a sense of competition. If someone believes that he or she should win, how can there be peace? We use the word *contradiction* to mean something negative, but we continually create contradictions within ourselves. We have to start within ourselves to create peace by training the mind.

Experts, your presentations are wonderful, but the picture is more complex. It is almost like seeing the tip of the iceberg, yet this is a very good start. With further investigation, discussions, and training, I think you will gain new insights through your research over the years and will be able to provide tools for people to become more calm and relaxed and no longer need tranquilizers or drugs.

Roshi Joan Halifax: I would like for us to reflect on our future and what His Holiness shared in terms of self-responsibility and the human mind.

From Johan Rockström, we learned about the profound issues we are facing on our planet, and that we are closer to the tipping point than previously understood. I would like for each of you to share what you feel we can bring to make a future that is more livable and compassionate.

Alexandra M. Freund: A part of our problem is that we view ourselves as being powerless vis-à-vis the tremendous problems on our planet. In a way, we feel that they overwhelm us and that we do not have the power to change it. The research on this feeling of powerlessness shows that it leads to inaction and the feeling that everything is futile. People say, "It does not matter whether I fly around the world three times or not; my actions do not matter. There are big companies that are spoiling the Earth." Some psychologists say that the constant feeling of not having power or a voice can lead to radical actions, which are truly destructive to oneself and to others, like terrorism, in order to be heard.

So, what can one do? I think we should remember what Johan shared about the ozone layer. By banning certain substances in refrigerators or in sprays, the ozone layer was repaired in a relatively short amount of time. This should empower us to take action and recognize that every person can make a difference when it comes to the environment. We can also improve our world by being respectful and caring toward one another. I know this sounds very optimistic, but I do not think there is any other way to start and initiate change.

Richard Schwartz: I was struck by what Tania said about the group that could not do the compassion practice. I would be curious to know how many of those people had a trauma history. I find that people who have been abused often have aspects of themselves that are frozen in those scenes, and it makes opening one's heart a very dangerous prospect. There are aspects of power within these individuals that prevent this from happening. I am afraid that the meditation community has not taken this into account enough when trying to bring more compassion. My philosophy is more of a constraint-releasing one. If you cannot open your heart, there might be some parts of you that do not want to, and they need to have a voice before you try to build up that muscle, or they might cause a backlash.

Markus Heinrichs: What we hope and aim for, in my field, is to develop new treatment strategies for individuals with severe social deficits. To do this, we have to understand concepts like power and care on the biological level and on the levels discussed here. I look forward to returning to my work now, to deepen our understanding of social behavior in humans, and bring more knowledge and information out into our complex world.

Tania Singer: I believe in the power of individual transformation and change. I love the work I can do as a scientist because, through developing and investigating these secular contemplative training programs, I can see how people, through relatively simple mental practices, can change without taking any drugs or costing a lot of money. I realize, of course, that even transformation is only taken in steps, but the power of people transforming from the inside is huge.

We heard about tipping points at the macrolevel. There are also exact, nonlinear tipping points at the microlevel. By cultivating certain qualities in yourself, the whole system can, in a nonlinear fashion, tip, and not to just the catastrophic end point, but also to real transformation. I would not underestimate the power of inner transformation, even on the microscopic level. I think the macrolevel and the microlevel are mirroring each other.

Of course, we need institutional change, and changes in our laws, but who creates our laws and designs our institutions? Human beings. If they do not understand from within, then there will be no outside force to change anything. With ourselves is where we have to begin. It is really the only responsible thing we can do because I cannot change you. I cannot easily change the government, but I can take full responsibility for my actions and for myself. I can set my intention every morning to change myself and become more conscious.

Roshi Joan Halifax: I thank you, Your Holiness, Dick, Alexandra, Markus, and Tania. I feel that we are opening up avenues of investigation that are important in trying to engender moral action in an imperiled world.

The Dalai Lama: Thank you.

Note

1. The *Bodhicaryavatara*, or *The Way of the Bodhisattva*, is a very famous text, still very much studied nowadays, and was written by the great sage and Indian philosopher Shantideva who lived in the 7th century CE.

III Perspectives from Spiritual and Religious Traditions

His Holiness the Dalai Lama commences the third session by sharing the role of religion in today's world: to promote peace and compassion. Maori elder Pauline Tangiora calls on behalf of the indigenous peoples to protect Mother Earth. Buddhist monk Matthieu Ricard relays the suffering on our planet, which is especially felt by those in positions of less power, and what it means to live a life of principled compassion for all species. The value of interreligious dialogue is elevated by human rights and environmental activist Rabbi Awraham Soetendorp, and Father Thierry-Marie Courau reflects on the value in being able to listen and to love without reciprocation. Lastly, Alaa Murabit offers her views on faith, and the need for more voices—from women, minorities, indigenous peoples, and youth—in order to provide representative interpretations of faith for a more caring future.

—Roshi Joan Halifax, Ph.D., third-session moderator, a Buddhist teacher, anthropologist, and abbot at the Upaya Zen Center in Santa Fe, New Mexico, USA

Opening to Part III

His Holiness the Dalai Lama

All Religious Traditions Carry the Same Practice = Love

One of my commitments as a Buddhist monk is to try to build genuine harmony among the different religious traditions. From Zoroastrianism to Judaism, Christianity, Buddhism, and Islam, all major religious traditions carry the same message: love. The practice of love requires the practice of tolerance, the practice of forgiveness, and the practice of servant discipline. All religions are doing these practices, and these are what form a shared basis for harmony.

Religions around the world hold different philosophical concepts and views. Theistic religions—Judaism, Christianity, Islam—have many concepts of the Creator, while the nontheistic religions, including Jain and Buddhist traditions, have no concept of a Creator, but rather self-creation—the idea that we create our own future.

In theistic religions, the concept of a Creator is wonderful: we are all created by one God, and that God equals infinite love. This concept gives the believer a feeling of close intimacy with God. If the believer sees God as the father of all people, if he is an angry father, it is difficult. But if the believer sees this father as a source of infinite love, it automatically brings the conviction "I am the son of God. I have the potential, because I share his genes of love. I am a part of him." This can be very powerful.

In nontheistic religions, Jainism places special emphasis on nonviolence and respect for all life. A Jain practitioner follows a strict vegetarian diet. Buddhism is like Jainism in that it emphasizes nonviolence. Buddhism speaks of self-creation, which means that all of your aspirations and experiences are entirely dependent on yourself. If you behave well, you will

benefit. If you do not practice compassion, there will be negative consequences. So, everything depends on you and nobody else.

Apart from the Creator or our own responsibility to build our future, if
one delves deeper, there are many other differences in the world's religions.
I believe these different philosophical views, traditions, and concepts are
necessary in order to pursue the practice of love and forgiveness in various
ways.

Different Philosophies Extend the Practice of Love

If one restaurant, from breakfast to dinner, always serves the same dishes,
the customer will most likely frequent the restaurant less and less. If there
is more variety, more people will come. Similarly, different concepts and
philosophical views are necessary to foster conviction about the practice
of love. This is why the Buddha himself also taught different philosophical
views.

Within Buddhism, there are four major schools of thought: Vaibhāṣika,
Sautrāntika, Cittamatra, and Madhyamaka. Within Vaibhāṣika, there are
also 18 different subschools of thought, each with corresponding scriptures related to the lay and monastic precepts of conduct, the Vinaya. The
Tibetan monastic tradition belongs to the Mula-Sarvastivada,[1] while Thai-
land, Burma, and Sri Lanka follow the Theravada tradition.[2] In China, there
is the Dharmagupta tradition,[3] and even that is divided into smaller forms
or traditions. So, one can see that even in Buddhism, there is a great diversity of traditions.

Cultural Aspects in Religion

Cultural aspects also account for differences in religions. A friend in India
told me that in the time period when Jain developed, there was a lot of
animal sacrifice, which is why the Jain masters especially emphasized veg-
etarianism. About 30 to 40 years later, Buddha came and also emphasized
the same things.[4]

In Islam, I have the view that the early Islamic peoples' lifestyle was
more or less nomadic. There were no proper rules. This is why, in the Koran,
special emphasis was placed on a set of precepts, which helped to bring
morality and discipline to these nomadic tribes.

In my own country of Tibet, in the past, the Dalai Lamas were also part of a system that was feudal in character. For a very long time in the Dalai Lama tradition, the Dalai Lama automatically held spiritual and temporal power. In 2011, I voluntarily stepped down from this dual responsibility, and along with it, put an end to a four-century-old tradition. I was happy to do this because the practice was very much tied to an outdated system. Everybody can now enjoy the wonderful democratic system. Democracy can also be too dependent on politicians, and although even democracy can sometimes be a bit complicated, I still find it to be the best system.

In India, the ruling elite created the caste system. This unhelpful concept asserts that, because of one's karma—which is, in turn, the work of a Creator—someone can have no rights. Similarly, elite people before the Russian revolution, as well as the French revolution, used religion to keep their power. What is religion? Love. Nobody is against love. But sometimes the system of a religion needs modifications to create a real possibility for religious harmony.

Living Harmoniously Together

India is good example of different religions living in harmony. All major world religious traditions have lived together in this nation of over one billion inhabitants for over 2,000 years. If religious tolerance is possible in India, why not then in the rest of the world?

Since the September 11 attacks, I am defending Islam. Muhammad's teaching and the Koran share messages that we must respect others' well-being, and others' rights. If an Islam practitioner creates some bloodshed, then the reality is that he or she is no longer a genuine Islam practitioner. Recently, during interviews, I expressed that the term "Islamic terrorist," or even "Buddhist terrorist," is wrong. This is because an individual who once is involved in terrorism is no longer an Islam practitioner, or no longer a Buddhist practitioner. This we should make clear. A terrorist is a terrorist. The very meaning of Jihad is not harming others in the fight for Islam, but actually a fight with one's own destructive emotions. That, I was told, is the real meaning of Jihad. I learned this from one of my Indian Muslim friends, and an Islamic professor in the United States later confirmed this.

If we take the first step to reach out to others, with conviction and effort, we can make more personal contact with each other. This way, we can reach out to fundamentalist Muslims, and even to some fundamentalist Buddhists. We are all human beings. We all die. Sometimes, circumstances create situations that require modification of the religions traditions. The proper way to do this is to reach out, consider others as brothers and sisters, and to talk. Through friendship, one can change—not by force. To encourage religious harmony is one of my main commitments until my death. Whether I am successful or not will depend on other people.

Let us be inspired by the different religious traditions that have evolved over the past 2,000 years. The Muslim population is about one billion. Christianity is also about one billion. There are around 250 million Buddhists in China and several more million in the rest of the world. Hindu practitioners number around one billion. These major religious traditions will remain. None of them can eliminate the other ones. It is therefore much better to live happily and be friendly, with mutual respect, and with mutual learning, which requires common sense and a wider perspective. With this, religious harmony is possible.

Notes

1. The Mula-Sarvastivada (2nd century CE) is a late school of Buddhism attached to the main Sarvastivada school. The tenets of this school of philosophy were first written down in Sanskrit and then translated into Tibetan in the 9th century CE. It is the root text containing and explaining the rules of monastic discipline (*Vinaya*) observed by Tibetan and Mongol Buddhists.

2. The Theravada, or "The Teaching of the Elders," is the oldest surviving branch of Buddhism that contains the words of the historical Buddha Shakyamuni as compiled in a corpus called the *Three Baskets* (*Tripitaka*).

3. The Dharmagupta school is one of the eighteen schools of ancient Buddhism. It contains a canon of monastic and lay rules (similar to those conceived by the Sarvastivada school), which are mainly practiced in China, Japan, Korea, Taiwan, and Vietnam.

4. Jainism and Buddhism were almost contemporaneous; both developed in the 6th to 5th century BCE in northern India. However, according to Jain cosmogony, this spiritual school would have appeared in the 10th century CE and would have counted 24 "Victorious Ones" (*Jina*) up to Mahavira (6th to 5th century BCE), the last major proponent of the Jain philosophy, who revived the main concepts and rules. Jainism is a religious school that emphasizes the respect of all kinds of lives, from humans to the tiniest insects, even including some minerals.

8   A Call from the Indigenous Peoples of the Earth

Pauline Tangiora

Opening Prayer
"Ka tangi te tiitii, Ka tangi te Kaakaa, Tihei Mauri Ora"[1]

In the language of my people, I first acknowledged the passing of all the people who have gone before us and who have gone in this short time. I also acknowledged His Holiness the Dalai Lama and all of you.

A Call to Protect Mother Earth and Her People

Power is given to all of us, to use for good or evil. Sad to say, as I sit here today, I see the power of the multinationals as they invade India. In the words of Vandana Shiva, they wish to take away the natural life of the seeds of the ground, of Mother Earth, so that the people in her area will no longer be able to grow seeds naturally.[2] Monsanto is coming into her country with genetically engineered seeds, which is not what the Creator has asked us to do.[3]

I think of the women, children, and men in the upper mountains of Colombia, and how these indigenous people are being threatened by a dam being built. Their sacred sites and their land are being taken from them for these dams. When we look at the Latin American countries, there is suffering in north Brasília, where dams are going in. The indigenous women, children, and men are lining up to stop these dams, for to take away the naturally running water of the rivers is to take away the heart of the peoples and their land.

We think of the people in many areas of Burma, where women and children are being put at risk by conflicts and merciless persecutions. The aboriginal women, children, and men of Australia, who have been there for six million years, are also in danger of being wiped out by multinational mining on their lands.

A Call to Protect Indigenous Pathways

All of these events have brought together the indigenous burdens that are being carried, but the power of belief, the Creator, is very important for indigenous peoples because the spirit of the land is in them and they are the land. The spirit of the waterways is part of them, and they are the water. Water gives life to all of us. When a child sits in the mother's womb, the water protects the child, and when that child comes, the water replenishes the land.[4] So, when we think of indigenous peoples, we think of the caring that they give and the responsibility they hold for the environment.

If we do not look after the environment, then we are no more peoples of the land, of the spirit of the Creator, because in creation, the spirit, which is given to each and every one of us, is very important to hold fast. In our land, we call it the *mauri*, which makes us who we are, and which we must always retain within us.

Sadly, the languages of the different indigenous peoples are being wiped out. Within the language of our peoples throughout the world, indigenous peoples have their storytelling, their prayers, and their songs, which make them the whole, and not just another group of people. We cannot allow this to continue.

When we talk about the power to care, indigenous peoples' lives—from the beginning to the end—are ones of caring in a community. Decisions are made within a community. They are not made in isolation, and a community is the one that nourishes and nurtures. Children go from family to family in safety in its villages, yet today, this is being threatened by outside influences. It is sad to see these influences taking priority. It is very hard for indigenous peoples to continue to walk on the pathway that they are born into because of pressures from the outside world. We hope that nonindigenous peoples will understand that indigenous peoples in this day and age must walk two pathways, not with anger or with disagreement, but in trying to understand the pathway of the European and the pathway they know, which is theirs by creation.

During my travels, it has been a privilege to meet the women, men, and children of the Sahara who have lost their land and are living in the desert because of greed. We must remember these people of the southwestern Sahara who are suffering, and the people in other African countries who are hurting through the greed of oil. We think of the Lakota people in America, who suffer because their land is being taken away from them by a multinational company. We must put all of these things into our basket and offer up in prayer that these will be resolved at some stage. We think of the Tibetan children who went over the mountains and their land being lost. What are we doing for these people? We have a global community. We must think of the others who do not have the power to remain on their land and be who they are as the Creator created us.

Today, it is not with anger or hurt that my voice is being put out on behalf of the peoples. It is because we love all peoples. We are created to be the guardians of the universe, and if we cannot practice this within, the world will die, the birds will stop singing, and the bees will not be there because the flowers and the bush will not flower anymore. All of these things are very important in the constraint of today's world.

A Call to Protect Our Relationship with Creation

We also have to remember that today's world is a world of technology. I am not an IT expert, but I see people with these computers and things, and they are always sitting there with them.

My little three-year-old grandson came to visit one Christmas, and he had never climbed a tree before because he lives in the city. I said, "Here is your tree. Climb it." He asked, "How?" I said, "Put one foot on top of the other." Now, that boy came back last Christmas. He said, "Nanny, I have to climb my tree one branch higher to get to the sky," and it was beautiful to hear him say that.

At nighttime, when Te Tairawhiti sleeps with me, I wake him up, and say: "*Harae mai moko*, Come, my grandson, look at the sky," and we gaze at a billion stars out of the window. "What are those, Nanny?" he asks. "Those are the stars of our ancestors," I respond.

We should do this more often with our children, tell them our stories of their ancestors, because without these stories, where will we be in 100 years' time, plugging away on computers? They do not tell the story. It is what the eye sees and what the heart feels.

Parents and grandparents out there, wake your children up in the middle of the night, let them go out and be a part of the Creator's creation, because without that, they will not ever feel what it is to be a part of the land, to be part of a universe.

Notes

1. This proverb refers to the blessed gift of life. It speaks of the voices of two birds in the forests of New Zealand. One (*tiitii*) has a quiet call similar to the name by which it is called. The other (*Kaakaa*) has a screech or scream. So, the proverb is likened to the quiet expectation of a pregnant woman and then the cry of a mother as the child is born. Finally, "Tihei Mauri Ora" is the sound of the child's first breath of life. This proverb is used by many Maori speakers across Aotearoa in formal speeches, so its ownership is thought to go back to the father of humankind named Taane Mahuta.

2. Vandana Shiva is an internationally recognized Indian environmentalist, writer, and feminist activist. She founded the *Research Foundation for Science, Technology, and Ecology* (RFSTE) which strives to combat international use of GMOs, pesticides, and fertilizers. In 1993, she was the recipient of the Right Livelihood Award.

3. Vandana Shiva, *Seeds of Suicide: The Ecological and Human Costs of the Globalization of Agriculture* (London: Zed Books, 2005).

4. This sentence alludes to the Maori tradition of burying the placenta of a newborn baby, thus regenerating the soil. This custom symbolized the fact that the infant takes his or her own place in the community.

9 A Life of Principled Compassion

Matthieu Ricard

If we were to summarize the very essence of Buddhism, it would be the union of wisdom and compassion. Wisdom is about understanding the nature of reality. Compassion is to wish to free from suffering all sentient beings who, through ignorance, are unable to recognize the way that things are and therefore suffer endlessly. They suffer because mental confusion and ignorance bring about hatred, grasping, lack of discernment, arrogance, and jealousy, which incite them to act in ways that are detrimental to others and themselves. It is only when wisdom and compassion are firmly established that we can think of growing power and using it, because then it will be used with the right motivation and for the right purpose: to bring as much well-being as possible to all sentient beings and to free them from suffering and its causes. Within the framework of wisdom and compassion, power becomes very meaningful.

The Goal of Buddhahood

In Buddhism, there is a very important concept called *bodhicitta*: the altruistic wish to achieve enlightenment in order to gain the capacity to free all beings from suffering. It begins with the acknowledgment that, right now, we cannot even deal with our own confusion and misery. We want happiness, but we do just the opposite of what will bring us happiness. So, how could we help others? We are like a beggar who wants to give a banquet to a hundred beggars with no provisions whatsoever.

According to the Great Vehicle, the purpose of achieving Buddhahood is to become a Buddha in order to carry on enlightened activities for the benefit of all sentient beings. Within this perspective, it is completely unconceivable to use power to harm, take revenge, abuse others, or exert power out of sheer arrogance, jealousy, craving, or greed. Any of these mental states and behaviors that are triggered by them will only bring about suffering.

Power Can Be Misused

Power itself is a tool. A hammer can be used to build a house or to destroy the same house. Ethically, power is also neutral. It does not hold value by itself. Care, altruism, and compassion, on the other hand, are not ethically neutral. Unambiguously, by nature, they are meant to bring well-being and to relieve suffering.

Unfortunately, power has a bad reputation. This is because it is quite rare for people to spend enough time to develop the wisdom and compassion to use power in the right way before they attain it. As it was mentioned earlier, power is not only brute force. Intelligence also gives us enormous power. His Holiness has often said that the people who were behind the September 11 attacks were extremely smart but used their intelligence for a terribly harmful purpose. With only a few tools and tricks, they used intelligence to bring immense destruction.

We, human beings, have exceptional faculties. Animals can do a certain amount of good and a certain amount of harm, but we are the only ones who can do immense good or immense harm. So, it is all the more essential that we do not use our unique intelligence to dominate, abuse, or oppress others. People in a position of less power—including minorities, indigenous peoples, and others—should not be abused by those who have more power. This also applies to the 8 million other species on planet Earth. The fact that we are smarter than they are does not gives us the right to use them as instruments of our selfish interests. Today, this typical abuse of power kills 60 billion land animals every year, or 6 million every hour, and 1,000 billion sea animals each year, or 120 million per hour. We kill roughly 100 billion animals in two months, which is more than the total number of *Homo sapiens* that have ever lived on Earth.[1] This domination is due to the blind use of power without and care and compassion.

Using Power for Good

Mahatma Gandhi is an example of someone who used power with compassion in nonviolent ways. We should not think that compassion is something that is weak, or just a nice utopia proposed by "goody-goody" people who cannot achieve anything, and that the best solution to quickly solve problems is to resort to violence. That is misleading. Satyagraha, Gandhi's movement, literally means "the power of truth," a power that can be used for justice, freedom, and equality. Such nonviolent power turns out to be extremely efficient. Some people also tend to see nonviolence as a weakness, but this is far from being the case. It actually takes much more courage to stand in front of an armed group of people who are beating people, like Gandhi and his colleagues did during the Salt March, than to go onto a roof, as snipers do, and shoot people dead. When His Holiness speaks of nonviolence to other human beings, animals, and the environment, this is using all of the power that we can have for the sake of goodness.

I would like to give an example with Tibet. His Holiness has systematically said that Tibetans should not use violence. But some people say, "Why not?" Is that the right alternative, to drop a few bombs, blow up a few planes? How could that ever help to foster the future harmony between Tibet and China, who will be neighbors until the end of time? There is no question about nonviolence being the better answer.

I remember, in Dharamsala, India, during one of the Mind & Life meetings, a person asked, "If someone comes here with a gun and starts to shoot everybody, and you practice nonviolence, what would you do?" His Holiness answered, "Well, maybe I would shoot him in the foot, and then go over and pat his head." Of course, the situation is not always as easy as that, and when people ask, "Are you not going to do anything if your country is invaded, if there is a genocide, and so forth?" the answer is, yes, of course we should prevent genocide by all means. But why do we wait for genocide to burst forth before doing anything? Why do we wait until the forest is on fire? How come we did not deal with the spark in nonviolent ways, through dialogue, education, and other forms of help? We could all see the genocides coming for a long time before they broke out, but we did not do anything about it. We had to bomb and send planes because we neglected to deal with the symptoms years before.

I remember being at the World Economic Forum in Davos with my dear friend, Rabbi Awraham Soetendorp. At a meeting of faith leaders, Archbishop Desmond Tutu said, "No religion ever could really condone killing." I said, "Great. Let's make a common declaration." And then everybody looked around and commented, "Well, you know, there are cultural differences, etc." The discussion was over.

Power Should Never Be Used to Suppress Life

In Buddhism, there is no excuse for killing. This is the ultimate use of power to suppress life. From the Buddhist perspective, there is no place for any use of violence or participation in war, and no difference between killing at war and murder. In fact, a soldier is fully responsible for those he or she killed, and a general is responsible for all of the killings that happened under his or her orders.

I do not know of any war that was waged in the name of Buddhism although there are plenty of examples in history of Buddhist people acting in barbaric ways and resorting to unspeakable violence. There was the Zen association with the militarism in the 19th century, there were the Zen kamikaze pilots during the Second World War, and the Khmer Rouge was also sort of tied up with the Buddhist institution. In Sri Lanka, the Buddhist institution sided with the government in oppressing the Tamil, and we know about the recent murderous oppression of the Rohingya Muslims in Myanmar, near the borders of Burma and Bangladesh. From a Buddhist perspective, there is absolutely no excuse for this. It is the same to murder someone in a time of peace or to kill someone at war.

Time magazine once published on its cover a story about killer monks, "The Face of Buddhist Terror," referring to a group of fanatics in Myanmar. I just want to remind everyone that, according to Buddhist perspective, anyone who kills, incites killing, or rejoices in it instantly breaks his monastic vows and is no longer a monk. There is no such thing as a killer monk; there are only killer ex-monks.

If we have full-fledged compassion, are guided by wisdom, and are inspired by sheer benevolence, then any amount of power is good because it will be used to remove suffering and bring happiness.

Note

1. Population Reference Bureau, "How Many People Have Ever Lived on Earth?," 2011 update, https://www.prb.org/howmanypeoplehaveeverlivedonearth.

10   We All Carry within Us the Rays of Light

Rabbi Awraham Soetendorp

Your Holiness, my brother, longtime friend, it is such a joy to celebrate our friendship, one which spans spiritual traditions and started only days after the Yom Kippur War in October 1973. As you said to me today, years on, "Our bodies may have aged, but our friendship is still as fresh as ever." This is the spirit of why we are here. We are here today to represent a secret, quiet revolution, where people from different spiritual traditions finally understand that we desperately need each other to achieve our common goal of justice and peace.

I would like to say a short benediction from the Jewish scriptures. When we are together in a unique moment, we say the following:

> Barukh ata adonai elohenu melekh ha'olam, shehecheyanu, v'kiyimanu, v'higiyanu la'z'man ha'zeh.

> Blessed art Thou, our God, source of all being, who sustained us, and kept us alive, to reach this moment. Amen.

The Power of Unity

Your Holiness, you are right to point to the unity and harmony of interfaith—it saved my life. Sira, my love, and I were war babies, and we were saved by the courage of people of another faith: the Catholic faith. My foster mother was, in addition, German born, and this awareness has carried me throughout my life.

Today is Shabbat, reminding us of the creation of heaven and earth, and the whole community of life. Today, we feel even more strongly the gift of the soul that God has bestowed upon us, which enables us to plant the hopeful future into the present and thus see a world filled with love and compassion.

Something extraordinary happened when God decided to create the human being on the sixth day. In the words of the Bible, the Eternal One said, *"N'assay Adam,"* let us create the human being. In one of the mystical commentaries, it says:

> God said to the angels, "Let us create human beings," but the angels said, "No, no, no, not human beings with free will. They will destroy everything." But, God said, "Yes," and after creating the first human being, he told him: "Let us create other human beings together." And God relinquished some of his own power to give humans beings more space, so that they would collaborate and be partners in this creation.

We still are partners in his creation—which is the most difficult experiment of all time. This is the meaning of the word *betsalmenu,* "according to our image." This is also plural, because it means that only when we allow everyone into the center of dignity—and do not push anyone away because of race, color, sexual orientation, or anything else—only then can we constitute, together, the whole image. In Islam, in Judaism, in Christianity, and in all of us, it says, "He who has saved one human being has saved the world. He who destroys one human being destroys the whole world."

How is it possible for people who are formed in the image of God to destroy, to kill, and for representatives of religion to engage in violence? We all carry in us the rays of light, as His Holiness has said: the gene of love of God. When we perform a good deed, we retrieve lost rays of light. And immediately those rays of light go back to their original source. One day, when we all engage collectively in the performance of *mitsvot,* "good deeds," and all of the rays of light are retrieved, the messianic time of peace will be realized. We are all responsible, together, to design and restore the world to what God wanted: a world of peace and justice, of power and care.

The Two Faces of Our World

The world seems to have two faces. One face is extraordinary. Never before in humanity have people gathered together to create anything like the Sustainable Development Goals, which say that, by 2030, there will be an end to acute poverty. As my friend Pauline Tangiora is rightly pleading, the Earth does not belong to us. This is stated in the Torah (Leviticus): "But the land must not be sold beyond reclaim, for this land is mine. You are but strangers, temporary residents with me."

I would like to tell you a short parable. There are two men in a boat on the ocean, and one of the men is making a hole in the boat. The other one said, "What are you doing; you are destroying us," and the man making the hole replied, "Don't worry, I am just making this hole in *my* part of the boat."

Johan Rockström's presentation was on hope. The planetary boundaries, where we can flourish, this is our boat, and we can do it? I wonder, can we create together a Council of Conscience, consisting of people who are moved by the many names of One God, the power names, and the caring names, who have earned our trust by their deeds, and help the United Nations Security Council to achieve security and a just peace in all the corners of the earth? I invite you to become one of the members of such a council. Because the other face of the world is threatening our future: the refugees who are crossing unfriendly borders and roaming the roads of often stern cities; the terror that kills, maims, and instills fear; the political deadlock and corruption that stifles human creativity; the unanswered longing of the soul for solidarity.

Here in Brussels, the wounded city, and in other places wounded by terrorism, we perceive the awakening of the firm resolve not to give up, and not to let go, but to harness the power to heal, from which we can draw strength and comfort. God demands from us to be true to our partnership in creation, to establish a world society in which no one is degraded.

To heal the world, we need to learn to use power tempered by care and compassion. We need to be present at the meetings of the powerful, like the G20, with the indomitable vision of mutual responsibility. We need to recognize that, when basic needs have been met, human development is primarily about being more, not having more. And to this cause of unity in diversity we must be visible in our friendship across religions.

My brother, Your Holiness, I remember what you told me years ago, when I spoke then about the struggle of Israel, which was at war, "Love your neighbor as yourself is the source of all of us," and I tell you, one day, Jews, Muslims, Israelis, Palestinians, Chinese, and Tibetans will all love each other.

11   To Listen and to Love without Requiring Reciprocity

Brother Thierry-Marie Courau, O.P.

Your Holiness, while listening to you, I realized that we have, in our hands, everything that we need for a better world. We do not need new ideas. Everything is already here.

Why do we not implement our ideas? Why do we not practice all of the things that we know would create a better world? Why do we seem to be more oriented toward the worst, and not the best? The "best" would be to make this world a happy place for all human beings, for all sentient beings, for creation itself, and for nature. Why, though, are we able to produce so many good ideas for the world, and, at the same time, are we able to do the worst?

The Caring to Listen and Serve with an Autocritical Mind

As religious leaders, we gain an authority by opening doors, giving access to another, better world. Maybe this is a shame for us. With this authority, people have also given us a power over them. Often, they want to see us on stage, in religious clothes, and honor us. They want to give their money, time, and life to the clerics. But they do not really care for what is at the true core of authentic religious leaders: to expand truth, love, wisdom, mercy, peace, and compassion. We must be aware of this. As religious leaders, if we do not exercise a critical mind on ourselves, we can become a danger to others by reducing them to slavery.

In Christianity, salvation occurs through Jesus Christ as the liberation of slaves, the reconciliation of broken relationships, and the transformation of practices of power. Disciples of Christ must take care of the power they receive. This power is not for the domination of others. It heals relational

MIND & LIFE
EUROPE

ruptures, restores, and reintegrates everyone in the community as brother and sister. It also establishes peace and unity, and it cares for others for free, without anything in return. This caring is, firstly, listening to others and serving people.

I like the Mind & Life logo. In it, there are a number of people listening to one another. There is a mouth in the ear of the other. Today, our world needs first to listen, only to listen, and not to discuss or debate. In the situation of listening, we are receiving the other as he or she is, without judgment but with compassion. So many people in the world need to be listened to, and only to be listened to! Even fundamentalist or radicalized people, most of the time, only need to be listened to, and to be welcomed and received as they are, with their violence. By listening to and serving the people, we take care of the world.

The Power of Choosing to Decide to Love

In other words, we can change the world if we choose to decide to love. I do not say to choose love. Every one of us chooses love. We all want love. This is easy. But what is love? Love is not a feeling at first. It is a willingness, a decision to orient our mind and heart to others and to receive them as they are. At first, love is a decision to receive and not a decision to give.

Often, we only give after grasping. I like this in the Noble Truths: the designation that one of the main attitudes of a human being is to be grasping, always grasping. Renouncing grasping, we become a receiver—of nature, of others, of sentient beings. We have decided to love. While we know that it is not easy, we have chosen. That is why we are entering into freedom. We are no longer alienated by the reaction of the other. If a rupture occurred previously, we become reconciled. Loving someone definitely, as he or she is, without waiting to be loved by him or her, we give up requiring reciprocity. "It is done! I have decided to love you, whatever you do!" This is why, if we can courageously decide to receive, listen to, and serve, without waiting for reciprocity, we could really make the world shine with love. In choosing to decide to love, we will be free and happy. The world will change, and the "best" will arrive.

12   Bringing Faith Forward

Alaa Murabit

We have been discussing power and care. Often, they are being termed as these elusive concepts, where they can impact one another, but are separate in their identities. Yet I see power and are as being one and the same.

Power and Care in Relation to Faith

For me, the first introduction to power and care, and particularly their intersection with faith, came from my own parents. My mother and father raised eleven children, of which I am the middle child. My father, who worked at the hospital as a doctor, showed daily sacrifice. My mother—if you ever want to see compassion, power and care, and justice exemplified, try raising eleven kids—was a daily embodiment of what my faith taught me, of what it means to be just and loving. My introduction to faith was not in a mosque, and it was not from somebody often glorified in religious circles—and this translates to all women—even though I consider my mother to be a religious teacher.

For a long time, faith has been a very exclusive domain, where the leadership is predominately male. Because of this, I believe that the policies created, which are very much in their likeness, betray a certain cultural and gender construct and change the way in which faith plays a role in our world today.

Interpreting Faith

There have been a lot of conversations about fundamentalism. I actually dislike that term because it somehow implies that these people are fundamentally of the faith; I think they are more deviant than they are radical or fundamentalist. I think this "deviantism" tells us a lot more about our state as a human people than it does about the state of faith.

Religion is much like power. It can be neutral. You can use it for the positive or the negative, and you can interpret scriptures in the way you see fit. You can dehumanize and belittle people, or you can elevate people. It is our interpretation that has resulted in a very conflicted world, where people of different faiths are excluded, where refugees—over half of which are children—are not allowed entry at the borders simply because of who they are, or for fear of what they "may do" in the future. I feel that we have not paid enough attention to the refugee situation and the ways in which conflicts have been dehumanized. We have equated individuals to security crises—we claim that it is not the migrants or the refugees that we are fearful of, but what they might bring. However, the reality is that this fear is often directed only at anyone or anything that does not look or seem like us. If we are going to delve deeper into the conversation on deviantism and extremism, be it Islamic, Buddhist, or otherwise, we have to start asking ourselves what it is in the structure or the institutionalization of religion that has allowed this to go on for so long. I think it is important for us to recognize that there are countries we are allied with that have funded and supported extremism for far too long. They have been key in transforming extremist individuals into extremist organizations and entities with political and economic power.

If half of the people born into faith end up leaving their faith before they turn 18, then we have to recognize that, while religion can be loving, compassionate, and kind, it can also be terrifying and violent. Our interpretation of faith can actually drive people away. Our interpretation of faith, our misuse of faith, the employment of faith as a tool for political and economic strength—rather than human compassion—is something that we have to address within our faith communities.

The Historical Roots of Today's Conflicts

It is wonderful and it is encouraged to always see the positive—the silver lining. This is another thing my mother taught me after raising eleven children. If we are going to step into a world where we can actually create interreligious dialogue and where we can all live harmoniously, then we have to accept the fact that there are historical roots to a lot of the conflicts that exist. We have to accept the fact that times in our history, like periods of colonization, have forever changed the way in which religion is interpreted in many parts of the world. It has changed the way in which we look at gender, race, and ethnicity. While I know that everybody likes to say, "The past is the past," we are our past, and without first recognizing the roots of the conflicts—both within our own faith traditions and among our faiths as they intersect—we will not be able to reach a solution where we can live in harmony and in peace.

Our Faith Has to Be Inclusive

The subject that I believe is most important when it comes to religion and religious interpretation is inclusion. While different perspectives and platforms are important, I think what has been lacking in interpretation, why power is misconstrued as a negative, and why power is always bombs and bullets is because power has been construed in a very masculine way. Faith has been interpreted in a very masculine way, and as a result, we do not deem compassion and care to be an inherent form of power. We view compassion and care as something separate from power, but I would argue that they are one and the same.

In order to truly exemplify power, and in order to define power, we have to recognize that a key component of it is compassion and care, and those are no less admirable than being able to shoot a gun—in fact, I believe they are even more so. Without the voices of women, minorities, indigenous peoples, and youth, we will not have representative interpretations of faith that are applicable in communities and which people can actually translate into their practical lives.

If we create a Council of Conscience, I think a key point on the agenda should be this: How do we take faith from being something in our textbooks—in the Koran, in the Torah, in the Bible—and compassion from being something we emphasize, to being applicable in the daily realities of our life? How do we make it into something we can actually translate in a world that is, unfortunately, exceptionally xenophobic and scared most of the time, yet very ready for a conversation about how faith can elevate compassion?

Dialogue with the Presenters, the Moderator, and the Dalai Lama

Roshi Joan Halifax: This is an opportunity for us to enter into dialogue with His Holiness.

The Dalai Lama: I feel there is genuine, deep mutual respect and friendship among us all. Recently, I was in Ladakh, India. It is a place where I feel that Muslims and Buddhists have very good relations. On this visit, I went to a Buddhist temple, to a Sunni Mosque, and to a Shia Mosque, to symbolize our close friendship.

In as early as 1975, I started paying my respects by making pilgrimages to mosques, in addition to churches, Hindu and Jain temples, and Jewish synagogues. On one occasion, in Delhi, after a meeting with Muslims from different Muslim countries, I went to pray at the great ancient mosque of Jama Masjid.[1] Wearing a white Muslim cap on my head, I prayed together with members of the Muslim community there. The next day, an image of me in a cap and praying was published in many Indian newspapers. I was a bit anxious about what the reaction would be from some Hindus, but later, a friend told me that many Hindus appreciated it. In Delhi, the Muslim community is not isolated but lives together with the Hindus.

Some Muslims also appreciate my teachings, which serves as further confirmation that we have the potential to develop the sense of oneness across all faiths. If it is possible in one place, then let us make a tireless attempt to achieve this on a global level. To start, we must spread our work. We need to plan more of these Mind & Life–type meetings in different places and reach out to other historically isolated Muslim countries. It will be a constant effort, like these meetings are, but they will bring significant, positive results.

Recently, I had the opportunity to meet some students from Islamic countries in the Middle East and Africa. Some of the young students had developed peace directly on the spot at an explosion where a friend or a loved one had died. At that very moment, these people developed the determination to work hard for peace. I admire these young men and women for their courage in a desperate situation. They do not have fear, they have determination and are making an effort to bring peace. I told them, "You are not alone, and every sensible human being on this planet is with you." The enthusiasm from these young people gives me more hope for the younger generation.

I would like to say a few words about indigenous peoples. In Canada, they use the word "First Nation." Maori people from New Zealand and the Sami people from Norway retain their religion, language, and songs and, at the same time, undertake a thoroughly modern education. I find this to be wonderful, and I feel that this is the proper way to preserve their own identity and culture. In contrast, the indigenous people in Australia still remain isolated, which, in today's world, is almost like suicide. I have visited Australia on several occasions; two years ago, I asked to go to Ayers Rock.[2] There, I met local indigenous people who lived in squalid conditions. A German person, with support from the central federal government, was carrying out an educational project to help them.

Since ancient times, indigenous peoples' cultures have been very tied to nature. Today, with modern society and modern technology, we sometimes have the perception that we can control nature. Ultimately, we are a part of nature, and for our own survival, we must respect our environment and find ways to live in greater harmony with it. Indigenous peoples can teach us a lot.

I would also like to say a few words about male dominance, which is present even in religion. A few hundred thousand years ago, human society was small. There was no education at that time and no concept of leadership. Because of this, everybody worked together and pooled whatever they could find to share equally. Eventually, the population increased. Farming started, and with it came the concept of my land, my possessions, in addition to stealing and bullying. The people said, "We need leadership." Since there was no education, leadership depended on physical strength. That was the start of male dominance. Later on, education brought more equality.

Today, we need to promote love and compassion. As previously mentioned, biologically, women are more sensitive about the suffering in others, so females should take a more active role in leadership so that, as a society, we will be able to promote love and compassion. With around 200 nations on this planet, I feel that one day, the majority of these nations will have female leaders. As a result, the world will have less violence. We have had enough of male dominance—men should now perhaps retire and relax.

Roshi Joan Halifax: His Holiness. Thank you for the cue. I think it would be wonderful for Pauline and Alaa to share, as a live example of women having the last word.

Pauline Tangiora: The last word must be for the future of our children. If we do not have the love of Mother Earth—because it is from the earth we came and to the earth we return—then we cannot look for a caring world for the future, and it is this future that we need to think about. We need to care for Mother Earth and Mother Sky, the land, sea, and forest, where we can go and pray and where we know we can survive in the universe. If we do not care for the universe, then we will not be here. But I know that the power of the love and the caring of you and me together, and the rest of the global population, will be successful for the youth of tomorrow. God bless you all.

Alaa Murabit: I wholeheartedly agree that we need to reconstruct our definitions of power and care. I would argue that it is not simply about being male or female, but what masculinity and femininity are. I think, both within and outside of faith, that we have to start challenging the interpretations, understandings, rhetoric, and leadership at times, which have created the existing construct that lends itself to misinterpretation and misuse. Women are ready to take on a much more active role, and deserve one, but we also have to challenge the structural inequalities, obstacles, and challenges that exist so that we can create a platform for anyone, first and foremost, in faith.

Notes

1. Located in Old Delhi, the Jama Masjid is the greatest mosque of India, built between 1644 and 1656, by the Mughal emperor Shah Jahan.

2. Ayers Rock, or Uluru, is an imposing rock formation in central Australia, located in the National Park of Uluru-Kata Tjuta, an area where many aboriginal ethnic groups, such as the Anangu, are living.

IV Perspectives from Economics and Society

The fourth session shares the age-old struggle between power and care in our financial and economic systems. With this, Dennis J. Snower presents his new work in Caring Economics, which explores avenues to promote personal and societal transformation. Sir Paul Collier imparts three stories about economics that reveal the flaws in the invisible hand. Bringing forward the female voice, Theo Sowa provides insights into the importance of valuing women's work. Lastly, Nobel Peace Prize Laureate Jody Williams presents PeaceJam, an initiative that helps to bring peace to our planet, as well as her successful campaign to ban landmines.

—Dr. Uwe Jean Heuser, fourth-session moderator, head of the Economics Department of the German weekly newspaper *Die Zeit*, as well as a professor at Leuphana University in Lüneburg, Germany

13 Self-Interest, Power, and Care

Dennis J. Snower

Your Holiness, there is a theme emerging through this dialogue that, while we are different human beings, we are all fundamentally equal and deserving of one another's care. So, the question is "Why don't we cooperate more?"

Two Visions of Human Nature

My question brings me to two visions of human nature. One vision is the standard, dominant, economic vision: *Homo economicus*. These are individuals who satisfy their selfish interests rationally through their choices. Another vision is Caring Economics, where humans are seen as being interconnected and multidirected, in the sense that they have a number of different motivations, which can arise under different circumstances (see figure 13.1). This view makes humans capable of power, care, and other motivations. The question is then "How do we move from one vision to the other, and what are the implications?"

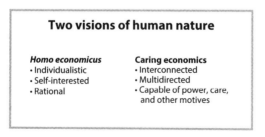

Figure 13.1
How can we move from one vision to the other for a more caring world?

The Nature of Cooperation under *Homo economicus*

Homo economicus is the basis of economics as we know it, and it explains cooperation to some degree. Why should we cooperate if we are selfish? Because we have synergies: we both stand to gain something when we buy and sell from one another. These synergies could explain why, over the past 50 years, the global production of goods and services has increased fourfold (see figure 13.2a). In addition, they could explain how nearly a billion people have escaped from extreme poverty since the 1990s (see figure 13.2b).

However, if we restrict ourselves to this narrow view of human nature, we cannot explain many of the major failures of humanity in modern times,

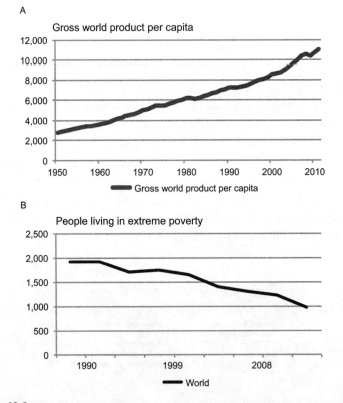

Figure 13.2

(a) Goods and services have increased fourfold in the past 50 years. (b) A billion people have escaped from extreme poverty since the 1990s.

including war, brutality, environmental destruction, overfishing, deforestation, and much more. There are two categories of failures. They can be driven by indifference and status seeking, such as climate change, resource depletion, and inequality. Or they can be driven by anger, animosity, hatred, or fear. This includes conflict, war, ethnic cleansing, and torture. The problem is that *Homo economicus* does not tell us enough about the human capacities we need to deal with these failures.

The Nature of Cooperation with Caring Economics

Caring Economics is the new paradigm that Tania Singer and I are developing. It sees humans as being driven by a number of different motivations, including power and care, and the context—often one's social context—is important in determining which motivation emerges. This means that we make our choices on the basis of our interactions with our environment, and this determines whether power and care become activated.

Three Motives: Self-Interest, Care, and Power

The motive of self-interest, which is what economists have focused on, suggests that people make each other better off through the purchase and sale of goods and services, and that—in the absence of externalities—all of the good and bad influences we have on one another are compensated materially. This means that people who provide benefits to others are rewarded for doing so, and those who impose costs on others pay for the damage. With the motive of care, including both compassion and loving-kindness, people impart benefits for which they receive no material compensation. This is the nature of altruism. As a result, people are positively interconnected. There is also the motive of power, which can be responsible for negative interconnectedness through status seeking, competition for positions in society, domination, and hatred. In this motive, people harm one another and do not face compensation for their actions (see figure 13.3).

We have done experiments around these motives, where people are given a choice: they can either contribute money to a common pot, where it gets multiplied, or they can keep it for themselves. People who are asked before the experiment to recall things that have made them caring contributed

Three Motives

Care	Self-interest	Power
Positively interconnected:	Asocial wants and needs	Negatively interconnected:
• Altruism		• Status seeking
• Compassion		• Positional competition
• Loving-kindness		• Influence and domination
		• Hatred
Positive externalities	No externalities	Negative externalities

Figure 13.3
The motives of care, self-interest, and power.

more to the common pot while those who recalled things that made them angry contributed less. This shows how motivations are important in driving people. Economics has been blind to this aspect so far. In addition, the experiment itself—contributing to a common pool of money or keeping the money for oneself—is viewed differently by caring people than by angry ones. The caring ones tend to see this experiment as an opportunity for cooperation whereas angry people see it as an opportunity to compete with one another.

What Makes Us Cooperative?

There are many forces at play in what makes us cooperative. In addition to synergies, where we make each other better off only whenever we both get something out of it, and kin selection, where we make one another better off only when we are biologically related and therefore seek to pass on our genes, I suggest that there are three other factors that make us cooperative (see figure 13.4).

1. The force of socialization
The force of socialization can take many different forms. The first is the influence of reciprocity: if I benefit you, then you benefit me, and, consequently, I have an incentive to benefit you. The second is the influence of reputation: if I am beneficial to others, then I gain a reputation for doing so, and others—who may not know me personally—will be helpful to me

What Makes Us Cooperative?

- Self-interest: **synergies**
- Relatedness: **kin selection**

- The Power of **socialization**:
    - Direct reciprocity
    - Reputation
    - Repression of competition
    - Behavioral norms
    - Moral values and virtues
- The power of **reason**
- The voice of **care**

Figure 13.4
A number of factors make us cooperative.

in the expectation that I will reciprocate. The third is the effect of suppression of competition: if we suppress opportunities to compete with one another—through law and order, progressive taxation, welfare state provisions, and more—then we become more cooperative since I can benefit myself only by benefiting others. The fourth comprises social norms and moral values and virtues, which can also ensure that I can succeed in benefiting myself only by benefiting others. All of these forces of socialization have a profound impact on our actions.

2. The force of reason

The force of reason makes us more cooperative when we treat each other as equals. It eliminates prejudices and alerts us to the long-term consequences of our actions. If we are in a community where we consider each other equal and do not have power over another, then reason can lead us to take each other's perspective. However, there is a major obstacle to the effectiveness of these two forces, socialization and reason. These forces are operative predominantly regarding our social "in-groups" rather than for our "out-groups," in other words, regarding our own cultures and societies rather than for those outside them. This problem is not shared by the next force.

3. The force of care

The force of care can overcome the disinclination to cooperate outside our social groups. The reason is that this force enables us to benefit from helping others, even when they reside beyond our national, cultural, and religious boundaries.

What Brings Us into Conflict?

We can be brought into conflict through competition for scarce resources, driven by self-interest and indifference toward others. Another source of conflict is our striving for status relative to one another. Beyond this, there are also the horrible conflicts that are driven by animosity, which commonly arises from four main sources: exceptionalism, dualism, victimhood, and dehumanization (see figure 13.5).

Exceptionalism arises when we think that we are more important and worthy than others. Under dualism, we feel we belong to the Forces of Good and are fighting the Forces of Evil. Under victimhood, we perceive ourselves as victims of the Forces of Evil, which requires us to defend ourselves and assert our rightful place in the world. Finally, under dehumanization, we see our enemies as evil.

If society would be sensitive to the sources of both cooperation and conflict—if these sources were investigated in schools and universities and if children at an early age were already aware of them—then we would be taking an important step toward healing this world. To promote transformational change, we must keep in mind that humans are social animals, that they often get their social identity from their own social groups, and that these groups may come into conflict with one another.

In Europe particularly, and also elsewhere, religion has been a big source of conflict. In the 17th century, after the Thirty Years' War, people

What Brings Us Into Conflict?

Humans are social animals, finding their social identity in groups.
Groups often compete and conflict.

Competition	Animosity-driven conflict
• Scarce resources	• Exceptionalism
• Gains from status	• Dualism
	• Victimhood
	• Dehumanization

Figure 13.5
Humans are social animals who find their social identity in groups, which often compete and conflict.

decided that they had had enough of religion and needed a different basis of identity. As a result, nationalism became important. However, this gave rise to the two world wars. Race became another basis of identity. It resulted in the Holocaust—the extermination of six million Jews in the Second World War. And in the decades before and after the world wars came the age of ideology, which brought about Stalin's Russia and the Cold War. All of these sources of identity can lead to conflict, raising the question "How do we get out of this, and how can we avoid it?"

Promoting Personal and Societal Transformation

In our research on Caring Economics, we explore two broad avenues to promote personal and societal transformation. One is internal change, through mental training practices. The other is external change, through social settings that bring people into cooperative relations with one another, promoting motives of care and affiliation. Social settings that are particularly effective in this respect are those that promote role reversal: we put ourselves into others' shoes, cognitively and affectively, thereby encouraging ourselves to build a common home. For instance, if we wish to promote role reversals with the refugees coming into Europe over the past years, then let us go to the refugee camps. Let us live among them and join them in common projects. Those who are engaged in policy making for the unemployed, incapacitated, unskilled, or other disadvantaged groups should live among them, in order to take their perspective. The legitimacy of policy makers should depend on their willingness to engage in role reversals with the people affected by the policy makers' policies. A prerequisite for agricultural policy makers should be perspective taking with regard to animals. There should also be school trips and public visits to abattoirs, so that people can understand the conditions in which animals are kept and then make their decisions concerning the foods they consume, bringing us a step closer toward building a common home with all sentient creatures.

In this regard, it is important to recognize the importance of a well-known ethical principle that is prominent in many world religions: "love of the stranger." Taking this principle to heart can bring us into harmonious interactions across cultural, religious, and national lines.

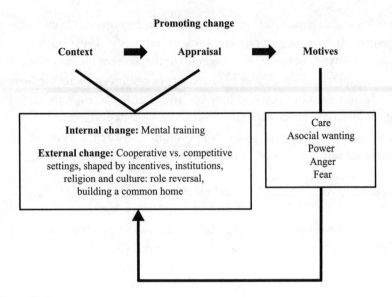

Figure 13.6

The Dalai Lama: Oh, wonderful!

Uwe Jean Heuser: Your Holiness, is there any reaction you would like to give us right away?

The Dalai Lama: I do not know. My knowledge about economics is zero. But I have realized, in the meantime, that economics is very important. One of my main concerns on this front is the huge gap between rich and poor. This is not only morally wrong, but also a source of a great deal of problems. While an economist works to further develop an economy, it is impossible to negate the sense of concern about other people, especially really poor people. That is why, where the economic system is concerned, I am a socialist, but even countries that are supposedly practicing a socialist economy are experiencing stagnation.

I was invited to Czechoslovakia by the late President Havel when it became independent. At that time, I expressed to him, "As the communist and socialist systems have more or less failed, and the Western, capitalist system also creates a gap between rich and poor, you now have an opportunity to create a synthesized economic system."

As far as my social economy theory is concerned, I am Marxist, because it stands for equal distribution. I admire that kind of ideology, but I must add that I am totally against Lenin, who spoiled the pure, genuine, compassionate spirit of Marxism.

Economists, you have the ability, while you are making more profit, to think about how to benefit poor people. Through what kind of mechanism, I don't know. You know better. Due to capitalism, it seems that the richer become richer while the poor still remain poor, or even get poorer. We have to think about that very seriously.

Dennis J. Snower: Bringing the voice of care back into economics will help in this regard.

The Dalai Lama: Very good. We are in agreement. Thank you.

Uwe Jean Heuser: Your Holiness, I think you were not quite honest with us. You know much more about economics than you gave yourself credit for.

The Dalai Lama: I am pretending that I know something.

Uwe Jean Heuser: The hope really is, that through Caring Economics and new approaches to human motivation, we can formulate economic policies that are different from what we have known. That would be much closer to the Third Way, which Eastern Europe never took, and maybe could not take.[1] Hopefully, there will be policies coming out of this research that can then be implemented across multiple societies.

Note

The Third Way is a philosophical and economic system that stands between socialism and liberalism; it advocates a synthesis of some right-of-center economic and some left-of-center social policies.

14 Three Economic Stories

Paul Collier

Your Holiness, I am going tell you three stories, and economists are not very good at telling stories. So, I will try my best.

The Story of the World According to Economic Man

The story of the world, according to Economic Man, goes like this. The world starts a terrible, greedy mess. Then, along come market forces. A hidden hand sweeps over the greedy, messy people, and low and behold, we are in an equilibrium, where all potential mutual benefits have been realized, once you have seen that hidden hand.

Now, this story is built on pretty shaky foundations. Dennis J. Snower emphasized the psychological aspects that this story misses in relation to different motivations: care and power, alongside greed and self-interest. What I would like to add is that the only form of interaction between the people in this story is through the market, but, actually, people interact socially way before they interact in the market.

Indeed, the things that economics takes as its starting point—individuals and greedy wants—do not fall down from Mars. They are socially produced and come out of social interaction. We saw in Sarah Blaffer Hrdy's presentation how a baby is born into a community and handed around. That baby will forge an identity and a set of values way before it develops the capacity for the rational calculation that economics assumes as its starting point. I understand from psychology that the capacity for rational calculation does not become established until the age of 14. By then, identity and values are largely already set. This means that we need to change our assumptions about motivation, and what is primary, and not the individual's wants.

Economics needs a revolution, and while economists are influential, they are also deeply conservative. So, where is the hope?

The hope lies in the fact that economists really envy physics, but the physics they envy is Newtonian, 19th-century physics. It is the world of billiard balls and the force of gravity. In economics, we wish that people were just billiard balls, and gravity is greed and incentives, or market forces. That is the world we are in. What the economists have not noticed in their envy of physics is that, about 100 years ago, physics moved on. Through its own revolution, it left behind classical mechanics and now has quantum mechanics. The core components of quantum mechanics are interactions and quanta—irreducible packets of waves. For interactions, read "social networks where people interact," and for packages of matter, read "identities packaged with values." This is where economics needs to go.

Let me turn to a second story, where we build a little bit of this in.

The Story of the Social Transmission of Values

What I am going to share with you is very new work. It is the latest paper by Professor Tim Besley, who is one of the world's most eminent young economists. This is absolutely cutting-edge mainstream. What is this story? It is a model, and like all economic models, it looks completely Mickey Mouse. So, do not mock it. Just try to get the little point that the simple model has in it.

The world starts a mess, as usual. What we are going to add is the social transmission of values—that is now going to be the invisible hand. The particular mess we want to start from is that America has too many aspirational alpha males, and so it is a rat race. Europe does not have enough of them. Everybody is so kind and gentle that the place is stagnant. America's aspirational alpha males want low taxes, while, in Europe, everyone likes equality, and so they like high taxes. Now, the aspirational people are happy in America, and the nonaspirational people are happy in Europe. That is the world we are in.

Regarding the transmission of values, the assumption is quite simple: children copy parents. What happens when you have a mixed marriage between an aspirational person and a nonaspirational person? Well, the child copies whichever parent is happier. In America, think of all those happy alpha males. The children grow up aspirational. The place starts a rat race, with too many alpha males, and over time, it gets more and more of them. In Europe, it is exactly the opposite. We start with not enough, and we get fewer and fewer. So, this invisible hand is there all right, but it does not take us to a happy equilibrium. It takes us to a divergent pair of "Hells on Earth."

Let me turn to my final story.

The Story of How Identities Come Packaged with Values

I am an Africanist, so I cannot resist ending with a story about Africa, and this is brilliant new research, not my own. It is about a factory that packs flowers in Kenya, and the factory workers are paid incentives for productivity. Economic Man loves this. It knows what is going to happen. It is going to be a happy outcome of mutual benefit. The one thing we add to that story of Economic Man is that identities come packaged with values.

Kenya has different tribal identities. Each tribal identity has its own values, which can include that some other tribes are considered enemies. In the packing factory, there is a mixture of workers from different tribes, but it is a line. The workers at the top of the line control the outcomes for the people at the bottom. When Tribe A gets to the top of the line, they deliberately mess up the flower packing. Even though it costs these workers lower pay, they do it because it sabotages workers from the other tribe at the other end of the line. Economic Man is missing that. There is an invisible hand. It is guiding us to an equilibrium outcome, and that equilibrium outcome is, again, an outcome from hell.

As these stories show, we cannot rely on the hidden hand. We actually need to learn to hold hands, and for that, Your Holiness, we need a teacher.

The Dalai Lama: Whether we recognize it or not, reality is reality. We are social animals—every human activity is related to the mind and to feeling, including the handling of money. Today's reality is that we are heavily interdependent across all continents, and I think our global economy is also part of this interconnection. As social animals, we need friendships that are based on trust, which comes by showing genuine care about another's well-being.

We all know that having a lot of money will not bring satisfaction or inner peace. It is affection that brings us deep satisfaction and happiness, isn't it? Think of very young children. They appreciate when their parents are smiling, and when they receive affection. Even animals are more honest when it comes to affection. Occasionally, humans consider money or power to be more valuable than human affection. I believe that a person who always thinks about money or power will die unhappy, with a great list of miserable experiences, while a person who has received a lot of affection will feel much more peaceful on his or her deathbed.

The economy, without human feeling, is something dry. What is the value of it? We have to use our intellect, and see that everything is connected to warmheartedness.

Paul Collier: Your Holiness, our subject has been indoctrinating students with a very shriveled view of humankind, and we are engaged in a battle to change that.

The Dalai Lama: Wonderful. Thank you.

15 Valuing Women's Work

Theo Sowa

Your Holiness, like you, I am not an economist. What I can offer to this discussion is my viewpoint from working with women and children around the world.

Our Economic Systems Value the Wrong Things

From my perspective, the economic systems and theories we are working with today value the wrong things, which leads to distorted perceptions and interventions. As a result, we end up with a world that is unequal and not moving in the direction we would like to see with regard to progress.

Our world is a world where people can sit in a room in New York or London and be paid millions of dollars or pounds to shuffle around pieces of paper, and, in doing so, make masses of people in other parts of the world hungry, poor, and less able to care for themselves and make progress in their lives. In this same world, we have people who raise and feed children, work in the fields, produce food, and make sure that communities are stable and yet are actively denied the resources to improve their lives in the way they want. For me, this is an example of a world where our value systems have gone completely wrong.

If we want to change the world, we have to change the way in which we think about economics, because economics is so powerful. Until we are able to change our thinking about what is valuable in our lives, and what gives it meaning, we will be held back and continue to invest in all of the wrong things. I do not want to be negative and say, "Economics is all bad. Tear it up, and throw it out the window." Economics can be a powerful force for change and for good, but only if it is used in particular ways and with good values at its core.

The Power of Women

I have personally seen from working with women, mainly in Africa but also across the world, that when women take charge of economics, they get really good results. In refugee camps, I watched how women organized themselves to make sure that the children had enough food to eat and were educated. In Liberia, I witnessed women, who, in the middle of a long conflict, organized the transport of food across the country to make sure that people in certain areas did not starve. It was these kinds of women who also brought the warlords to the peace tables and made them negotiate. Even when I look at academic research, I come to the same conclusions: one report on the Ivory Coast showed that to get measurable improvements in child health, education, and nutrition, one needed to increase a woman's income by US$10 a year. A man's income had to increase by US$110 a year to achieve the same results.

Valuing Women's Work

When it comes to the contributions that we should be valuing when we assess the progress of a country, too often, we discount a large area of work—women's labor.

There is a certain type of work where we say, "Yes, this is work, and we will pay people a lot of money to do it." Then, there are other types of work where we say, "That's not really work. It is just what women do," and a lot of this work is in relation to care.

I would like to tell you a story about a film I saw a while ago. It was about a woman who woke up at about five o'clock in the morning. She got food ready for the children and started to clean the house. When the children woke up, she got them dressed and ready for school. When her husband woke up, she gave him breakfast and made sure that he had food to go to work with. After he left, the woman took the children to school and then made sure that there was water, food, and whatever else was needed. She then started to cook the dinner. She cleaned the house and went into the garden to make sure that the vegetables were growing well. She then picked up her children, brought them back home, did their homework with them, cleaned them, and got them ready for bed. That evening, her husband came home with some work associates. As the woman served dinner to her husband and his friends, the husband introduced his wife to the guests. They asked, "What does your wife do?," and he answered, "Oh, nothing. She is a housewife." All of the wife's work and contributions became nothing because of this distorted view.

This distortion of women and our work also happens within the economic sphere. When governments decide where to invest money, too often they make the wrong choices. People are telling them, and they are also telling themselves, that to be a lawyer is more important than other types of work (like raising children or caring for family), or that to be a hedge fund manager brings greater value to the economy than some of the work that women do, particularly when that work (as market women, for example) is referred to as being part of the "informal" economy. As a result, when it comes to investments to progress economies, I think we are investing in the wrong things, and I see this a lot, not just in Africa, but across the world.

Women's Work with HIV/AIDS and Ebola in Africa

I would like to share another story, about the role of women when it came to HIV/AIDS. People now are talking about a world in which HIV/AIDS can be stopped altogether, but for many years, in many parts of Africa, HIV/AIDS was like a plague. People, communities, and economies were dying. Now, the reversal of the spread of that pandemic was partially about being able to obtain the right medicine at the right prices so that people could be treated, but a lot of it was also about social change.

It was the women of Africa, especially grandmothers, who, after watching their children die, decided that instead of sitting back, they would adopt their grandchildren. These women also went to their neighbors who had been dying and took those children into their homes. They then went into the neighboring villages, found the orphaned children, fed them, sent them to school, and brought them up. These women had no money, but they made sure that this happened. As a result, African societies, which could have crumbled, lived. It meant that communities, which could have died, did not die. Yet, when people tell the story of HIV/AIDS, what these women did to turn the pandemic around is rarely told. As a result, when people invest to prevent similar kinds of health catastrophes, they are not investing in the work that women do.

Recently, we saw this again with Ebola, a disease that devastated three countries in West Africa. The international story was that Médecins Sans Frontières (MSF) saved those countries. Now, I love the work of MSF, and they were wonderful because they were there when other people did not want to be there, but the people who were the first responders in that Ebola crisis were the women of Liberia, Guinea, and Sierra Leone, and they get no credit for their work. Yet MSF and others could not have been successful in their work without the initial and ongoing work of the women of those countries in the so-called care economy. Again, when the international community later decided where they were going to invest their money to help those countries recover, and also to look at prevention, on the whole, they forgot the women and subsequently invested in the wrong areas.

I do not know how many times we have to learn this lesson. We see the work of women and the change that they bring, and yet, over and over again, we ignore or trivialize their work.

Women's Work Needs to Be Recognized

Lastly, my work has shown me just how powerful women are. Very often, when people talk about power, they speak of a power that comes from being in positions of authority or about people who have lots of money or own lots of guns. Yet, women have an inner power that is absolutely enormous. Every woman has, within herself, the opportunity to make a choice to use her personal resources, brain, body, and heart for good, for change, and to push toward equality, but we need to work toward a world where these opportunities are made more possible rather than quashed.

Every time we ignore women's power and women's agency, we are allowing the world to continue down a path of negativity, waste, and destruction, instead of onto a path where everyone can work together to create the kind of communities we envision. I am not saying that women should do all the work; women already do too much work. What I am saying is that we need to recognize and value women's work—both the formal and the informal, in the home and outside of the home. We need to have our economic systems account for it, so that we can invest in the right ways and give it the profile that it deserves. This will enable us—as children, teenagers, and adults—to look at the world in a more equal way.

As a world, and as an international community, we should value, recognize, and reward all types of work that women do and all of the economic contributions that women make. Doing so will help lead us to the kind of world that we really want.

Notes

1. John Hoddinott and Lawrence Haddad, "Does Female Income Share Influence Household Expenditures? Evidence from Côte d'Ivoire," *Oxford Bulletin of Economics and Statistics* 57, no. 1 (February 1995): 77–96.

16 Creating Change with PeaceJam

Jody Williams

I primarily work on women's issues through the Nobel Women's Initiative, which is made up of six female recipients of the Nobel Peace Prize. We have come together to use whatever influence and access we have to help create change by supporting grassroots women's activism in countries that are primarily in conflict around the world.

When we created the Nobel Women's Initiative ten years ago, I finally liked being a recipient of the prize. I feel that the Nobel women "share" the Nobel Prize with grassroots women activists and shine a spotlight on their work so that others will know the work that they do. The fact that none of the 94 men who have received the Peace Prize ever created a Nobel Men's Initiative says something about how different men and women are.

Creating Agents of Positive Change with the PeaceJam

I would like to talk about the joint work I am doing with His Holiness for PeaceJam, an organization that was founded nearly 20 years ago by Dawn Engle and her husband, Ivan Suvanjieff—a punk rocker from the American band The Ramrods. This couple had the idea of bringing Nobel Peace Prize Laureates together with youth to show young people that they have the ability and the power within themselves to participate as agents of positive change.

PeaceJam has made a massive difference in the lives of young people around the world. We have done different PeaceJam events in nearly 40 countries. This PeaceJam in Brussels marks the launch of a ten-year effort in Europe to counter extremism, hate, racism, and isolationism, and serves to help young people know that they can seize the future and make it different.

A Call to Governments to Unite Instead of Divide People

When I look at the things that cause conflict, and what might promote change, there is one big thing that is missing in our governments, and this is promoting inclusion and bringing people together in common cause. I believe that governments actively promote anger, fear, and the belief that there are others who are not as worthy as we are. This, in turn, promotes racism, sexism, and hatred of lesbian, gay, bisexual, transgender, queer, questioning, intersex, and allies (LGBTQQIA) groups of people. When a government wants to keep and promote its power, it is done by dividing people and by making fear the major passion of the day.

I believe that after the 9/11 attacks in my country, the United States, when President Bush, and members of his administration such as Cheney, Rumsfeld, Wolfowitz, and Rice decided to illegally invaded Iraq, and started calling everybody who was not "us" a terrorist, this unleashed global terror. The government wants to focus on ISIS, and on the Syrian refugees who are sneaking "terrorists" into the West, and put a negative twist on the things we do not understand. The government is powerful in making this happen, and if it can make you afraid, it can control you. This is seen in Europe, where there is confusion about the massive migration of people from the Middle East, and in the United States, with presidential candidate Donald Trump telling Mexico—a sovereign state—that he is going to build the wall between the countries and make Mexico pay for it. This is seen everywhere now.

As we have seen in the last few years, it is phenomenally easy to divide people. Once you have, it is very hard to bring them back together again. It can happen, but it takes dedicated activism by people who refuse to accept the notion that people are different and are unafraid and willing to stand up to governments.

We talk about the terrorism of Muslims, and ISIS, Boko Haram, and the Somalis, but what about state-sponsored terrorism? When my country uses drones against countries with which it is not at war, to me, that is terrorism.

PeaceJam takes on what is driving people apart in our world today by working as a powerful tool to help heal divisions and to change the feelings of isolation and hate. I believe that if we want to promote change, we have to help the youth. People need to understand that we have human responsibilities as well as human rights, and if we do not stand up and participate in change, we are complicit. As I often tell my students, complaining with your friends about things that you think are wrong is not a strategy for change. This is the first PeaceJam in Europe. The plan is to have it grow throughout Europe and reach ages from 5 to 25 years old. I have even done a PeaceJam in kindergartens. It scared me to death. It was so hard to find what to say to those little people.

Bringing About Change for Everybody

Last night, we went to the Brussels municipality of Molenbeek and had a session with 15 young men and women. They were just like me: they want to be active and do good in the world. They are creating projects, which include bringing sports equipment to the Ivory Coast, so that they can work with young people. Even in the face of the discrimination and isolationism, they are thinking beyond the self and their Muslim community in Belgium. These young people see themselves as human beings in the world and are working to show that we are all human beings, that it does not matter if you are black, white, red, yellow, or brown or if you are from Africa, the United States, or India. It does not matter. We all want the same things.

People resort to violence when they feel that there is no choice, and that no one will listen. Governments need to listen to what young people are saying and do something about it. It cannot just be "a dog and pony show"—governments cannot be permitted to trot out nongovernmental organizations (NGOs) created by the state when it is convenient to their story. There has to be a genuine partnership between government, civil society, and international organizations to bring about change for everybody.

I want to bring about change for everyone, even the people I "hate." I am no Mother Teresa. To me, the "Love your neighbors as yourself" business really means do not kill them. You do not have to invite them to your house for dinner, but it means to accept and respect their way of life.

Dialogue with the Presenters, the Moderator, and the Dalai Lama

Uwe Jean Heuser: Jody, in addition to the PeaceJam, you have led one of the most impressive movements in caring about something very destructive, landmines, and you were very successful. Could you share what you did that made it possible to bring about change?

Jody Williams: Through our landmine campaign, we have done assessments and have tried to help people understand how to build a global movement. Our campaign started with two organizations: one in the United States and one in Europe. This enabled me to call it "The International Campaign to Ban Landmines," which was a useful tool for growing it. Ultimately, we had campaigns in 90 countries and about 1,300 NGO members.

We developed an annual framework for reaching our campaign goals, but we never forced any member to participate. For instance, if an event or activity made sense to our Cambodian members in a given year, they would participate; if it did not make sense, they would not. This made the movement free-flowing and flexible although our message was always very clear about what we were striving for.

In the campaign itself, we talked about a treaty; we talked about governments giving money to get the mines out of the ground—because they sold them, gave them away, and put them there; and we talked about money for helping landmine survivors. Billions of dollars have been given by governments so far, and this is all because civil society said, "Enough. We are not going to sit back and let these mines continue to kill people," and they can kill for up to 100 years after the end of war.

We also did not have a rigid leadership structure, which was empowering. Everybody in the campaign brought unique talents to it, and people participated in whatever capacity they could. A couple of women were fabulous at slogans. In five words, they could explain what was going on in the discussion about landmines. Other people made incredible displays. At one meeting, there were piles of shoes to represent people who had lost a limb and no longer needed a second shoe. We also had people who could write and others who could talk. It was not an ego-driven campaign, which I think is partly why it has been so successful.

The reason that this landmine campaign has been the most successful arms control treaty in history is because the campaign continues. There are meetings with governments every year, and if governments are not doing what they are supposed to do, they are gently pushed. When I have spoken with others about the campaign, I have refused to speak to people "in their uniforms." I would tell them, "Take off your military uniform or diplomatic suit and think about what is being said in terms of if your own family lived in the middle of a minefield." Since we could not bring these leaders into a minefield in Cambodia, we brought the minefields into the meetings by building them in front of the meeting room doors with sensors. When you stepped across and touched the wrong sensor, there would be a blowup sound, and it was scary.

The most important thing to me about being able to create change is to make people accept that we all have power. Either we choose to use it, or we remain silent and abdicate our power by giving it to people who are willing to use it. If you do not feel you have power, you are going to sit there and feel defeated.

Uwe Jean Heuser: Theo, this is also one of your subjects, individual power, and how to put it to good use. Many people have a lot of power—also in the economic realm—and some use it for changing the world, like Melinda Gates, while others choose to speculate with food prices on a global level in order to make more money. What can we do so that more people, including leading economic figures, use their power to create a more caring economy?

Theo Sowa: I think it is important to get the masses to first understand their own power and then to use it. I think we have been very good in this world at minimizing people's sense of their own power, and yet, when you see power being used for good, it is really amazing.

When people talk about philanthropy, we tend to think about the big names, the big givers, and I am very happy that Bill and Melinda Gates are putting money back into the community, as there are a lot of very rich people who do not give a cent. When people give, we should always give them kudos, yet ordinary people probably give far more of their everyday income than some of the famous people that we talk about.

In the UK, there is a campaign called Comic Relief, which raises between 60 million and 100 million pounds every couple of years from the British public. Money is raised from normal people giving five pounds here or a pound there. Children go to school wearing red noses and get a pound from their teachers. Now, these people who are giving five pounds might be giving a much bigger percentage of their income than, say, someone like Mark Zuckerberg, or Warren Buffet, or any of the other big names we have.

My real push is how do we, as people, give enough visibility to the good that people do, every day, in all kinds of circumstances. How do we make people understand the power of five pounds from someone who has four children and is living in conditions that are nowhere near those of a multi-millionaire? Part of it is about our learning to listen better. We need to treat people's ideas, challenges, and visions with respect. I think, when we act collectively, we can get the majority of this world to tap into their power and decide to use it for good, and this will enable us to push those leaders who prefer not to see the more difficult ways of moving forward. It is sometimes easier to put everything into a box and say to people, "You do this. You do that. I know what is good for you, and this is the way we are moving forward." It is a lot less complicated and a lot less messy than allowing millions of ideas to flourish and saying to people, "Ok, let's use that energy, but for that energy to be positive, we will have to work collectively, so that we can actually push those people who hold the levers of power that they are not using constructively at the moment."

Uwe Jean Heuser: Paul, you raised the question about inequality, which has been taken to unbearable dimensions. How can we reduce inequality?

Paul Collier: I think there are two very different challenges to this. The challenge that I have spent my life working on is how the poorest countries can catch up to the richest. This is a huge struggle, which is not being properly engaged with. Over the next ten years, I think this is actually going to become much more serious, because a lot of the poorest countries had a good decade, but it was quite a lucky decade. The prices of their exports went up for a while; now they have come down again. A lot of the good news is over, and so trying to sustain catchup through the next decade will be really hard. We also need a much more serious and focused approach for the poorest countries. At the moment, I am trying to work with the G20 countries. The next G20 will be in Germany [in 2017], and there is a good chance that there will be quite an initiative on helping Africa to increase its investments to catch up.

I think it is a very different question about inequality within countries. The reality is that, over the last 20 years, a lot of poor countries have started to catch up, but within the richest countries, inequality has gone up, and so while global inequality has gone down, the inequality in rich countries has gone up.

For a long time in the 19th century, a distinction was made between the deserving and the undeserving poor. We all know that this is unwise, because poor people are very often not poor by their own fault, but even in the rare cases when it is their own fault, they need help. They need care and compassion. I have come to believe that the distinction between the deserving and the undeserving makes more sense among the rich because there are a lot of rich people who have not earned their money in a way that has benefited other people. They have earned their money through what economists call "rent seeking" and ordinary people call "plunder." We have just not made this distinction yet. There are innovators and entrepreneurs who have done a lot of good for all of us and have deservedly enriched themselves in the process, and then there are people who are making money by being smarter than ordinary people. The financial rent-seeking sector has mushroomed in the last 20 years. We all have money in pension funds, which are run by ordinary people who are not as smart as the smartest, and the smartest are plundering and outsmarting our pension fund managers. They are enriching themselves at our expense. This has not been properly addressed.

Uwe Jean Heuser: Dennis, when we talk about actions, like putting more responsibility into the financial sector or trying to differentiate between deserved and undeserved riches, the government comes into play. Does the government play a role in your framework?

Dennis J. Snower: Yes, the government is in our framework. The government, in the standard economic models, is the institution that provides monetary incentives to get people to do what they otherwise would not do. In the wider understanding of the world inspired by Caring Economics, the government also provides settings in which people can be drawn either into care and cooperation or into division. One thing that our analysis will hopefully do is alert people to when the government is being divisive and when it is bringing people together within and across national boundaries. This is important because we now live in a world that is economically integrated and socially fragmented. The bottom line is that it is people who elect governments, and if the people are socially fragmented, then the government will only be elected by mirroring and leveraging that social fragmentation.

The big challenge is how to raise the voice of care among the voters. Governments can provide settings for doing so, but the voters themselves need to be keenly aware of the opportunities that role reversal and building a common home can provide, and also the pitfalls that lead toward conflict.

Sometimes, people see themselves as victims. The big challenge is for these people to recognize and overcome their victimhood and not repay harm with harm by foreseeing the cycles of violence that would otherwise arise.

Conventional economics is basically blind to all of these issues because economics is only concerned with self-interest. It is not concerned with doing good to others or harming others. Through our analysis, we are able to give governments a much wider capability for influencing our future than was conceivable before, because they can build institutions, as well as identify narratives and norms, that will bring people together, and provide settings where people can cooperate.

Uwe Jean Heuser: We live in a world where there is more and more knowledge about the caring side of humans and their interconnectedness. These are things that Buddhists have known for a very long time. Today, this even influences economic thinking, yet it seems that the real world is still going in the other direction, with more and more inequality within countries, with very fierce competition, and with financial markets going crazy. So, my question is: "How can we turn this around? How can we apply the knowledge we now have to direct the world more toward caring? How can we bring about more internal and external change?"

The Dalai Lama: All major religious traditions emphasize the practice of compassion and love through different approaches. In Buddhism, particularly in the Nalanda tradition, extensive use of reason is emphasized, whereas, in other traditions, the willingness and enthusiasm to practice compassion comes mainly through faith.

Whenever I meet people from the media, I mention my three commitments: promoting a sense of oneness in humanity, creating religious harmony, and preserving Tibet's environment and rich cultural heritage—which I describe as a culture of peace, nonviolence, and compassion. I often remind media people of their important role and responsibility in promoting a sense of oneness in humanity, in addition to religious harmony. When the media only report murder, rape, and corruptions, people get the impression that basic human nature is very negative, but basic human nature is actually positive. It is important for the media to share more about our inner values by not only reporting the negative side. This way, we can achieve a greater balance and see our future as hopeful and good.

Our existing educational system is oriented toward external values, and when it comes to inner values, historically, people saw religion as carrying the responsibility. Today, however, regardless of whether one is a believer or a nonbeliever, we are all part of a greater whole. For us to attain maximum benefit for humanity, we need to improve our education on moral principles from kindergarten up to the university level, so that we can create happier individuals, families, communities, and a happier world. In today's age, we need a more universal approach to teaching key human values and ethics within our secular education system. My hope is that, by next year, we will have a draft of such a secular educational curriculum that focuses on the teaching of these universal values. Education is our basis for hope, not prayer.

On one occasion, in the Bihar State, in India, the chief minister invited me to the opening ceremony of a Buddhist temple. There, the minister mentioned that with Buddha's blessing, his state—which was quite poor—may rapidly prosper. I responded, "If Buddha's blessing can make your state prosper, then it should have much earlier, because Buddha's blessing has already been around for over 2,500 years." I then continued, "Buddha's blessing must go through the able chief minister's hand."

The government is important. In order to choose the right person, people need to see the reality, and the media play a very important role in this. Through education, we can reduce threats and increase the importance of caring.

The time has come for the promotion of human love and compassion. Females have a special role in this regard, and so I ask all women to have confidence and to please make an effort. With your innate sense of compassion and humility, you have the potential to help us all. My first teacher of compassion was my mother, by showing genuine affection. I think my siblings and I never saw my mother's angry face. It was always compassionate and peaceful. My father had a short temper, and so he occasionally gave me physical "blessings," which made me have a more negative feeling toward my father.

Each one of us has the responsibility to make an effort to change the world. Change must start from one individual. When I see the problem our humanity is facing, I hear people say, "I don't have the ability to create change." But who will start? Do we start by praying to God? Sometimes, I jokingly tell people this: "Muslims pray to Allah, Christians pray to Jesus Christ, and the Buddhists pray to Buddha to bring peace on this planet. If we have the opportunity to see Muhammad, or Jesus Christ, or Buddha and ask for peace, I think the response will be 'Who destroyed peace? Who created violence? Not Buddha. Not Jesus Christ. Not Allah.' No. We created that."

Rabbi Soetendorp spoke about God giving responsibility to humans in the process of creation, and that some angels were worried that it might be too risky. This is a good explanation. A few years ago, one of my Indian friends, a very religious-minded person, asked me very seriously, and very sincerely, "If God creates our entire humanity, and God is merciful, then why are there misused people among his creation? Why did God create this?" I had no other way to answer but to say, "Since God also created hell, there must be some people who are ready to go. Otherwise, there would be no meaning in its creation." You see, all of these human-made problems are our creation. We have the responsibility and the logical capacity to solve these problems, and not through prayer. Through the power of prayer and the power of blessing alone, I am quite skeptical, really.

Please, everyone, think about how you can make your own contribution for a better world.

V Personal Commitment and Global Responsibility

In this fifth and final session, art is portrayed as a vehicle for creating direct personal experiences and illustrating social and environmental issues with Olafur Eliasson. Scilla Elworthy shares her powerful work to prevent nuclear war, her business plan for peace, and suggestions on how we each can contribute to peace in our world. Frédéric Laloux enlightens us on the new organizational frameworks that are emerging, which are self-organizing, transparent, and collaborative.

—Theo Sowa, fifth-session moderator, CEO of the African Women's Development Fund in Ghana and an independent advisor and consultant in international social development

17 Art as a Driver for Social Change

Olafur Eliasson

Sphere, shown in figure 17.1, which I created for the Power and Care conference, is powered by a small solar panel on the roof. What is glowing in this sphere is actually the sun shining outside. It is not a functional light or a pragmatic solution, but rather an emotional story about the light and power outside of this room. When I talk about the world, I believe it is important to explain it not only in functional, pragmatic terms, but also in emotional, nonquantifiable terms.

Figure 17.1
Sphere, 2016, artwork installed at the Power and Care conference.
Photo: Petter Hoff/Studio Olafur Eliasson

Art That Hosts Great Diversity

As an artist, I have long been interested in what types of space, and what types of artwork, can host great diversity. The sunlike installation at the Tate Modern in London in 2003, shown in figures 17.2a and 17.2b, invited people to become part of a work of art themselves. Instead of suggesting that art is on the wall or on the floor, it became the whole space; you could not separate yourself from what is art and what is not. This allowed people to do all sorts of things. More than two million people visited this exhibition, and many used it as an opportunity to express themselves. What was interesting was that people shared this space and acknowledged that they were not having the same experience. This meant that the fact that you and I might not fully agree on what we were seeing could serve as an amplifier to our friendship. In a world where most spaces seem to allow only polarizing arguments that lead to one party's

A   B

Figure 17.2
The Weather Project, 2003, at the Tate Modern
(Photographer unknown)

Figure 17.3
The Collectivity Project, 2005, building a new civil society in Tirana, Albania.
Photo: Albes Fusha

members having to leave, spaces of culture make it possible for people to be together without having to fully agree on everything. This makes art a great resource.

With the project in Albania, at the Tirana Biennial in 2005, shown in figures 17.3a and 17.3b, I invited people to come and share what it is like to build a society by working with Lego bricks on a big table to create a type of city plan. After a few days, a boy, who was usually selling cigarettes on the street, was at the table. The policeman, who was normally busy chasing this child away, was at the same table, discussing with this boy whether a house should be like this or like that.

In hosting diversity through art, I have also worked over the years with many experimental scientists and mathematicians. In the late 1990s, I was very inspired by phenomenology, which led me to Francisco Varela, Michel Bitbol, and Evan Thompson. This interest led me to collaborate closely with scientists. Some of our experiments were successful, and some were not (see figure 17.4).

Figure 17.4
Model Room, 2003. This image provides a view into Olafur's studio during the time he
was working on phenomenology-inspired projects.
Photo: Jens Ziehe

Making the World Accessible through Art

Making models of the world is very much about making the world accessible.
At COP21, also known as the 2015 Paris Climate Conference, politicians,
scientists, and people who work with big data came together to discuss climate change. While these meetings are very important, the people outside
of these meetings can feel disconnected from the discussion. They may say,
"What do I know? The ice is in Greenland; it's so far away." So, I came up
with the idea that if I could show the Greenlandic ice in Paris, in the center
of the city, people would walk up and look at this ice and immediately connect to touching a glacier in Greenland (see figure 17.5).

For this installation, we shipped 80 tons of ice to Paris. It gave us the
opportunity to make the nonquantifiable, emotional narrative from the
science about climate change accessible to people in a second (figure 17.6).
Our future, of course, is central here, and these images show that there are
many ways to touch ice.

Figure 17.5
Ice Watch, 2015—blocks of ice from Greenland at COP21.
Photo: Martin Argyroglo

Figure 17.6
Ice Watch, 2015—Children in Paris making friends with Greenlandic glacial ice.
Photo: Martin Argyroglo

Feeling Included through Art

With art—whether it is a theater play, a great book, a film, a piece of music, or a dance performance—you can have an experience where you all of a sudden say, "I know that feeling. This is me." It reflects a not-yet-verbalized, subconscious, emotional need. You might say: "It is as if this piece of art saw me; it spoke on my behalf; it is expressing what I want to say, which means I am not so bad after all. I am OK. I am good enough. I went to a museum not to see art but to be seen by the art; by the museum." When people walk out of the exhibition, they feel reflected.

The word "inclusion" has great gravity. I think that culture has the power of inclusion on many levels. On the caring level, it reflects people's emotional needs, so that they can say, "I am a part of civil society. I can be a part of civic trust."

Through the creation of this Little Sun solar panel lamp, I was able to combine power and care (figure 17.7). On the one hand, this light is a

Figure 17.7
Little Sun solar-powered lamp.
Photo: María del Pilar García Ayensa/Studio Olafur Eliasson

practical thing. It is an LED. On the other hand, it is something that makes me feel connected and interdependent. It holds sunlight, making me feel like I have my own power station. I am powerful.

Light is not just about getting things done—it is also about happiness. It is about how I feel and whether my day offers me the opportunity to do nonquantifiable things, like read, have a party, or dance. We see these solar lamps in a classroom in Paris in figure 17.8a and at a school in South Africa in figure 17.8b. In trying to create a language about what unites us, what

A

B

Figure 17.8
(a) Students with Little Sun lamps in Paris. *Photo:* Max Riché. (b) Students with Little Sun lamps in South Africa. *Photo:* Tim Feherty.

feelings we share, I came up with the idea of bringing light to where there is no access to energy. One billion people in the world do not have access to energy—that is one in every seven human beings. This means that they use petroleum or fossil fuels as their primary light sources, which is bad for the climate and for respiratory health. This lamp serves to change this by providing an affordable alternative at the grassroots level with everybody sharing a little bit. Lastly, in Nepal, just after the earthquake in 2015, a huge effort was made to provide access to energy after power stations collapsed and failed. These solar lamps enabled work to go on into the night and provided the comfort of light at a time when there was a lot of darkness.

Theo Sowa: Thank you so much, Olafur, for beautifully weaving art and culture into the theme of power and care, and for your ability to actually drive change.

The Dalai Lama: A beautiful presentation. As a Buddhist practitioner, I find it to be very different from a scientific presentation that is driven by data. Wonderful. I think this shows that your brain is something very creative, which is good.

18 Finding a Way to Put an End to War

Scilla Elworthy

Your Holiness, I would like to share with you what I am passionate about at the moment in terms of personal commitment and global responsibility.

My Work to Prevent Nuclear War

For the past 40 years, my work has involved my spending hundreds, even thousands, of hours listening and talking to those who have a great deal of power over nuclear weapons. This includes those who design the warheads in the laboratories; those who strategize to deploy the weapons, the military; the intelligence community, who give the rationale for the weapons; the people who sign the checks; as well as the political leaders who have the terrible responsibility of putting their finger on the trigger. In my work, I have listened to people from all of the nuclear weapons nations: the UK (my own country), France, China, the United States, Russia, India, Pakistan, and Israel. I have never spoken with someone from North Korea. In 2001, I started to work at the grassroots level with people who risk their lives daily so that other people do not get killed in areas of hot conflict like Colombia, the Congo, Zimbabwe, Sri Lanka, Nepal, and Northwest Pakistan.

In my work, I have discovered that all of these people, the research community that I work in, and the military as well, now know so much about how to prevent war that we do not need weaponry anymore. This is especially so because the threats that humanity has brought about—from climate change to migration, even terrorism, and the gap between rich and poor—do not respond to weapons. Perhaps this is an evolutionary moment, a challenge, for us as human beings to upgrade our level of consciousness and our way of preventing war. To clarify, I am not talking about conflict because conflict is just energy—it is not good and not bad. What I am talking about is the destructiveness, the terrible legacy, and the debris of war.

A Business Plan for Peace

What I am doing now, along with my colleagues, is putting together a plan, at the local, national, and international levels, for what ordinary as well as powerful people can do to prevent war. It is a business plan for peace.

To create this plan, we first laid out what it is that makes war continue, which is not just the military-industrial complex that everyone speaks about that obviously makes a fortune from weaponry. It is also those who are comfortable with a war situation because it means that they can traffic weapons, drugs, and money. For these people, we have to recognize that the continuation of war is in their interest. If we are going to deal with such violence, we have to understand how the people who are invested in war think, and that is why I am interested in listening and in speaking with them. For over 25 years, we have organized dialogues in Oxford, Beijing, New Delhi, Geneva, and Moscow to bring war decision makers together with informed critics—people who were once in the business of making weapons, who know the details, and have stepped out of their role.

We know a lot about how much weapons cost, but not so much about the detail of what it costs to *prevent* war. In working on our study, I found that, on the ground, the grassroots cost to prevent war is US$1 for every US$1,885 spent on the weaponry required for war. The latest information from the Global Peace Index of the Institute for Economics and Peace in Australia states that the economic impact of armed violence on the global economy is US$13 trillion. In our first study of the cost in our business plan for peace, we worked out that to efficiently and effectively prevent war at local, national, and international levels would cost merely US$2 billion.

How We Each Can Create Peace

I would like to share two examples of what ordinary people can do to promote peace. First, people can insist that their children are taught to meditate at school. Secondly, people who live in countries of conflict can insist that their governments build an infrastructure for peace. This is what Nelson Mandela put into place when he was released from jail. It included a national-, regional-, city-, and village-level peace council. On these councils are respected individuals from the community, and their job is to make a peace plan for that community. This only costs US$2 million to set up for an entire country.

The Dalai Lama: I appreciate what you have to share. What you are doing makes information available to everybody, so that that humanity can prevent nuclear war from happening.

Two years ago, there was a Nobel Peace Prize Laureate meeting planned in Cape Town, South Africa. When I was refused a visa, in order to show solidarity, the venue was shifted to Rome. At the event, some of the Nobel Laureates and organizational representatives were working to ban nuclear weapons. Experts in this field were explaining that if nuclear war takes place, there would be a nuclear winter, or a nuclear holocaust. We all listened to the terrible scene they described. I then suggested that we make a time plan, within two years, to make the world free of nuclear weapons. Everybody looked as though they were in full agreement, and yet nothing happened.

If we can explain nonviolence, with discussions led by Nobel Laureates, the banning of nuclear weaponry could become more than an aspiration. It could become a worldwide movement, mobilizing masses, countries, and the world. I believe that the Japanese people are totally against nuclear weapons and would form part of the movement; the European continent might also be receptive. We need an individual, like you, to take the lead and suggest different organizations to join in, and eventually the United Nations and governments.

Scilla Elworthy: People need to make it impossible for the politicians not to act.

The Dalai Lama: At least a free country can express its voices strongly and publicly. People will listen. America has the most powerful arsenal of nuclear weapons. What if America would start this kind of movement, then point it to Russia, China, and North Korea? Any major nation with nuclear weapons can unanimously decide to do something. I believe it is possible for this world to be free of nuclear weapons. In a second step, we should reduce offensive weaponry. For many years, I have had the dream of a European Unified Force. I wish this also for Africa, where independent sovereign states are killing each other through useless and senseless wars.

If we can start this movement, I think it will be possible, through education and awareness, to bring an end to war. What is the use of war? It brings destruction, more suffering, and pain. I believe that humans have common sense, and that human basic nature is more compassionate.

Please inform people how serious war and the killing of human beings is. Please also share that the use of this weaponry creates tremendous destruction. It is a total waste of money. I think about those brilliant scientists who used their ability for killing.

Scilla Elworthy: They could be designing things that make life better for people.

The Dalai Lama: This has been one of my dreams for a number of years.

19 Power and Care in Organizations

Frédéric Laloux

Your Holiness, I would like to speak about power and care in the organizations where most people work every day: in businesses, nonprofits, schools, and hospitals.

A new way to hold power and care seems to be emerging in the world right now. Everywhere, at least in the Western world, people are becoming increasingly disillusioned with the places where they work. More and more, managers are leaving their businesses, nurses and doctors are leaving their hospitals, and teachers are leaving their schools because the places where they work and the way power is held there hurts their integrity and feels inhospitable to the longings of their soul.

I believe, in many ways, that this a good sign. I think we are seeing an old system dying and a new system starting to emerge. Quite a lot of psychologists and philosophers have written about this new consciousness, including Robert Kegan, Jenny Wade, and Ken Wilber. We know that what is developing is on an individual level, as people grow into new ways of looking at the world. My research has focused on seeing how this new system is affecting the organizations in which we work.

New Organizational Frameworks

I have been researching organizations that have been founded or led by people who had often done some inner or spiritual work, and from the perspective they gained, the normal way to structure and run an organization no longer made sense. As a result, these people started to experiment, and in the process, discarded everything they had learned in business school. After much experimentation, what each of these organizations ended up with was often remarkably similar, not just in the principles they used, but even in the concrete everyday practices. It seems that, at the same time, different people are formulating new, yet similar, ways to structure and run organizations.

In my work, I have looked at a number of organizations and have chosen to study organizations across all industries and geographies with at least 100 employees that have been operating according to these new principles for at least five years. To my surprise and delight, a number of organizations met these criteria. Some had 100 people, some had a few thousand, and others had more than 10,000. I even found very large organizations already operating for up to the past 40 years with these radically new ways to hold power and care across all kinds of sectors and industries.

These organizations are very different from traditionally run organizations. One big difference is the way in which they talk about the organization. In our current, scientific, materialist paradigm, people tend to refer to organizations as a "machine" (see figure 19.1a). Actually, it seems like a machine is our metaphor today for nearly everything, including the human body and the world. Consistently, these new organizations use a different image. They consider themselves a living organism (see figure 19.1b). This change in image has profound implications, and it comes with at least three fundamental breakthroughs.

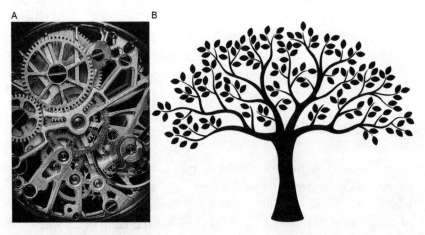

Figure 19.1
Machines serve as a common metaphor for traditionally run organizations while new organizational frameworks consider themselves as living organisms.
Photos: (a) Bednarek/123RF; (b) Mujiono/123RF

Self-Organizing Systems

The first breakthrough is the way that power is organized within these new organizations. The traditional pyramid, with a boss and then layers of hierarchy, does not exist. What now emerges are organizations with thousands of people that operate in self-organizing ways, entirely without any levels of hierarchy, without anyone being the boss of anyone else, and without anyone being subordinate. It may sound impossible, but the most complex systems in the world are natural systems, and they have been operating like this for billions of years. The human brain, with its 85 billion cells, or just any one cell, or a complex ecosystem like a forest, all operate in a self-organizing manner. What is extraordinary is that different people are simultaneously figuring out how to import these principles that have operated in nature for billions of years into our organizations.

This way of operating radically changes the nature of power in an organization. There is no longer "power over," but instead "interconnected power," or "power with." And there are enough of these organizations out there for us to know how this works on a practical level. We now know the structures and processes that are needed—how to make decisions, do practical things, pay raises, and handle conflicts—when there is no boss.

Living into Wholeness

The second breakthrough is that, as these organizations reveal, there are two ways to look at the world: from a place of fear, separation, and scarcity or from a place of love, connection, and abundance. In most organizations, because there are subtle fears, employees find that it feels best to be separated and wear a mask and to not show one's deepest concerns and longings. In my research, I have found that when we show up behind a mask and only show a small part of ourselves—the part the feels safe and acceptable—that we are also only showing a small part of our energy, creativity, and passion.

These new organizations look at work as a place to live into wholeness. They have found ways, which some spiritual traditions have known for thousands of years, to create a safe space, where it feels safe enough to show up with all of who we are and to discover who we are in a way that is incredibly caring. Employees in at least three of these organizations said, "Sometimes I wish my home was more like my work," because there is so much care, and because they have consciously created this safe container for people to show up whole. Again, we already know how to do this. There are a number of things that need to be upgraded, starting with basic human resource processes, as this is typically the place where fear starts with recruitment and yearly evaluations.

A Sense of Purpose

The third breakthrough that we learned from these organizations has to do with purpose and how we look at the future. In today's mechanistic view, we need to predict and control the world. Accordingly, organizations have strategic plans including five-year plans, yearly budgets, and targets. But people in these new organizations say: "That no longer makes sense to us. We believe that the organization is not a lifeless machine that we need to program. It is a living organism that has its own kind of destiny or energy that it wants to manifest in the world. Our role, as leaders, is much humbler. It is simply to listen to where this organization wants to go, and to just go with it." None of the organizations I researched, all of which are spectacularly successful, have a strategic plan. Instead, they have different ways to listen to where the organization wants to go, and we now know how to do this.

This new, emerging consciousness provides practical ways to shift to a new way to bring power and care into organizations. As a result, it radically brings more life, power, purpose, and meaning. This is not a theory or a model. These are real organizations out there, and more and more are popping up. I feel this is a message of hope for all of us who are leading or participating in an organization, a school, a business, or a hospital. If something hurts your integrity or your soul in the way that things are run, there is inspiration out there for you to start to run things differently.

The Dalai Lama: Wonderful.

Theo Sowa: Frédéric, could you please provide one practical example of an organization you worked with?

Frédéric Laloux: In the Netherlands, there is a home care organization called Buurtzorg with nurses who visit and care for patients, often older people, in their homes. This is such an interesting and beautiful story because it shows the traditional, "machine" way to think about this care in an organization and then the "living organism" approach.

In the 1980s, the machine way to think about management took over in Holland. The Dutch state, which is paying for the nursing services, thought: "To increase savings, let's make all of the nurses that work independently become part of an organization, so that we can have economies of scale." When they forced these nurses into large organizations, a whole new logic took over.

Managers of these organizations then thought, "Oh, these nurses still have their personal clients, which makes it difficult to fill their days. Sometimes, they have gaps between two clients, which is costly for us." So, the state created a call center, took away the phones from the nurses, and set a new system in place, where clients did not have their personal nurse but instead someone who was close by and free.

Then, the state realized that the experienced nurses were more expensive, so they decided to give them the complicated work, and the rest was done by cheap nurses just out of school.

"Some nurses are faster than others," they then realized, so they allocated times to each task: giving a shower cannot exceed 15 minutes; a shot takes 10 minutes; changing a compression sock, 2.5 minutes.

The state then decided that it would be good to create a planning department. As a result, each nurse received a sheet of paper that says, "You start at 8:00. You change the compression stocking. You are out again at 8:02. Google map calculates that it takes six minutes to drive to the next client. Then, you give a shot, which should take ten minutes." In response, the state said, "This is great. Now we can do continuous improvement," and so they asked the nurses to put barcode stickers on the front doors of their clients' homes and to scan them when they went in and out.

With all of these developments, the managers had the ability to look at all of the data and say to a nurse, "You know what, with showers you always lose one or two minutes, so we will train you on how to give more efficient showers."

That all makes sense from the point of view of the machine paradigm. Why would you not do it? It makes things cheaper, so that more people can be helped. Yet, those in the middle of this, the clients and the nurses, were miserable. Imagine the client: often, it is an old person who is somewhat confused. Every day, there is a new nurse coming in, and the client has to re-explain everything. The nurse looks at his or her paperwork and says, "Oh, you need a shot," and the client says, "No, I called the doctor—things have changed a little bit," and the nurse responds, "I'm sorry—I have no time," and injects the shot. This setup also deeply hurts the nurses' integrity because they often know that they do bad work, but they have no time.

In the middle of this, one of these nurses, Jos de Blok, said, "I cannot take this. For me, the purpose is not to give efficient shots, but for patients to live rich and autonomous lives," and so he set up Buurtzorg, which means "neighborhood care." With his company, the nurse takes time to sit down to drink coffee with his or her patient, and asks, "What is it that you can still do in life? What is it that you can no longer do? Do you have children? Oh, your children don't help you because you don't get along. In that case, could I help to you reestablish dialogue?" It is amazing what nurses do in this organization.

The organization goes back to a model where one person just sees one or two nurses and they develop a beautiful, deep, caring relationship. Buurtzorg, which was founded ten years ago, grew from 4 to 14,000 employees and went from zero to 70–75% of market share. Because all of the nurses want to work for them, they receive over 250 job applications every week. What is most astounding is the financial aspect of Buurtzorg's work because you could say, "Of course it is easy to give good care if you drink coffee, but we are trying to optimize every minute." Buurtzorg only uses 40% of the hours prescribed by doctors because patients become autonomous so much faster. So, it is a total paradox to the organizations that try to squeeze every minute out of work. If you drink coffee, you are actually saving the Dutch state hundreds of millions of Euros every year.

Buurtzorg's 14,000 nurses are all organized into teams of ten to twelve nurses with no team leader. They have a tiny headquarters with 50 people and have no head of finance, no head of human resources, and no marketing team. Everyone is incredibly caring. Also, the nurses help each other out when they encounter problems or emotional difficulties when working with terminally ill patients, and they have formats to do this in ways that are marvelous.

Hopefully, this gives you hope, a glimpse into and a sense of the work this organization is doing. Notice how the nurses and the patients are the same; the only thing that has changed is how this organization views the world.

The Dalai Lama: Thank you. I am very impressed when an expert describes these kinds of processes. Time is always moving. Many organizations, including religious organizations, look more or less like a hierarchical system. At its top are dignitaries who act more or less like despots. I think people have the impression that an organization that is authoritarian, and controlled by one person, is more effective, even though this goes against basic human nature.

I think that your work is wonderful. At the same time, when I think of our planet of seven billion human beings, and their different experiences, wishes, and ways of thinking, I feel that it would be almost impossible to create a system where every participant is going to be totally happy. That is human nature. (Laughter)

According to Buddhist philosophy, everything is interrelated. In a lot of these organizational structures, we have to take into account the relative context in which they are operating. There is no such thing as the absolute or the best. But I really congratulate you that you are not content with the existing system and try to make improvements, which is most welcome.

Dialogue with the Presenters, the Moderator, and the Dalai Lama

Theo Sowa: I would like to ask Olafur about the power of art to change people's views of the world. What has your experience been?

Olafur Eliasson: Art has this ability to allow you to be involved with critique and, at the same time, also reflect upon your own potential. Great art informs us, but really fantastic art listens to us. This is why it is important to see culture as one of the pillars of our societies.

Making and experiencing art has a lot to do with questioning. "Am I connected to the world? Do I feel interdependent?" When I make a drawing and it is successful, I feel that the pencil on the paper is, in fact, pushing the world, and I feel connected. When the drawing is not so focused, I feel disconnected.

When experiencing a work of art, the caring component comes through when you realize, "Oh, this is how I feel! Now I see myself in a bigger context." This particularly applies when you are part of a cultural festival and are suddenly in a situation where there is space to express your views openly, and where not everyone agrees. It creates a safe haven in culture and teaches us that disagreeing can even be a quality, an amplifier. In the political and cultural sector, these spaces are done with great success and art contributes to society this way. It is also important to recognize that there are artists in every community, people who are teaching and working with children, telling people, "Some things are hard to verbalize. Let's have confidence in the emotional language that art is." Art is a language, and what gives it quality is not how we make art, but rather what we say with art.

Theo Sowa: Could you each share something from this dialogue that you will take away with regard to your own personal commitment to global responsibility? What do you hope the audience will take away?

Frédéric Laloux: One thing that has stood out for me in this conference is that the distinction between being people who are powerful and those who are powerless is a very real one. On another level, it is not true at all. We have heard some beautiful examples of people who have suddenly stepped up and changed the game. The example I gave is Jos de Blok, the nurse. There are thousands of nurses in the Netherlands, yet he decided to take action. What will stay with me is a new way of looking at the world. There are structural imbalances, and let's not negate them, but I will look differently at being powerless. For me, it is a call for action: "What is it I can feel called to do, and how scary would it be to step into my own power?"

Theo Sowa: And for the people who have been on this journey with us for these two days?

Frédéric Laloux: I would offer the same: "What prevents each of us who hear a voice different from the mainstream to act? How beautiful, scary, and wonderful would it be to step into your own power?"

Scilla Elworthy: I will take away the evident power of the feminine in men as well as in women. The question I ask myself is "How do we provide practical things to do, so that everybody can make this world a more peaceful place?"

I have a question for His Holiness: How do you see the feminine principle, the Yin, and how that can be brought back into balance with the masculine, the Yang, which, in our world today, is very much out of balance?

The Dalai Lama: I always consider the ultimate to be love and compassion— a genuine sense of concern for the other's well-being that is not mixed with attachment. What I mean is that the ability to share love and compassion is not determined by what others think of you, or the notion that if someone is kind to me, I will extend my love—this is biased. It also does not matter if you are a religious believer or a nonbeliever, or if you believe in the next life or not.

Love and compassion without attachment or partiality is the belief that we are 100% the same as everybody else; that we are all sentient beings, including insects and fish; that we do not want suffering; and that we all have a right to achieve a happy life. With this understanding, a sense of concern develops, and a kind of compassionate attitude that can also extend to your enemy. Only we, human beings, because of our intelligence, have this ability; animals do not.

By taking care of ourselves, and by understanding the workings of our mind, we can develop a more compassionate way of thinking that enables us to take care of others, which brings maximum benefit for us all. On the other hand, the more you think about yourself with a narrow-minded or self-centered attitude, the more problems and trouble you create. By viewing the world this way, we see that each individual life very much depends on society, and society very much depends on the whole world: humanity. Ultimately, for your own interest, you have to generate serious concern about the well-being of others and the whole world.

Modern education started to develop with the Industrial Revolution, which has made it very related to matter and oriented around material value. Yet, the human mind is not a machine, but something far more complicated, which is why our education should start with the basic human nature of our mind. I do not know how to go about doing this, but I do know that, through education, we can develop a deeper and larger awareness. This is why I have asked some experts to draft a curriculum. From this, I believe more compassionate power will come.

We are so used to viewing one side of power, to control, but power is something much more than this. It is both positive and negative and even neutral. To reveal this, we need broader research work.

As you can see from our presenters, our research can be considerable and very precise, which is remarkable, but it does not capture the whole in terms of seven billion human beings. We are complicated, and the real troublemaker comes through our intelligence and emotions, which are special abilities granted to us as human beings. If these abilities make us look at things as being complicated and problematic, it is better to pray that the end of the world comes soon! But this would be silly. On the other hand, if we can use these abilities to develop infinite altruism and to take care not only of ourselves, but of others—including our children's children and all the different animal species and the environment itself—then we tap into what makes human life precious and what makes humanity worthwhile to be saved.

I am now more than 80 years old. Perhaps in 15 or 20 years I will not be here, so I do not need to worry very much, but many of you are younger, so you will have to look more seriously at this, because you will live for another 30 or 40 years. (Laughter.)

Humanity is confronted with a lot of challenges at present. Now is the opportunity for each of us to make a contribution, through our professional work and in our own personal lives, to achieve a happier humanity and a more peaceful world.

Conclusion

Tania Singer

It is with gratitude that I wrap up the Power and Care Dialogue. From science, we know that gratitude is emerging from the same biological/psychological system as compassion, loving-kindness, and care, and it is always a wonderful opportunity to practice these qualities.

In thinking of how I could possibly integrate the richness and multiplicity of what has been shared, the image of Olafur Eliasson's art piece, *Sphere*, came to mind. Olafur's art instillation was created especially for the Power and Care Dialogue. Close up, the solar-powered sphere consists of a multitude of little glass-mirrored triangles, which are reflecting light and perspectives to each other. One could think that this sphere is just an addition of a lot of little different, separate parts, but if one looks at it as a whole, it is a unity, a new gestalt, an art piece. It is a sun, empowered by the real sun shining outside. Olafur's *Sphere* serves as an image, or a metaphor, for this dialogue, by showing that we are much more together than each one of us is as an individual: we form a new gestalt.

The Power and Care Dialogue has brought together a multitude of perspectives, creating a kaleidoscope of voices. Starting from an evolutionary and anthropological perspective, the conversation dove into hormones, down to the very microlevel of oxytocin and other, low-level neuroscientific aspects. From there, it moved back up to the perspectives of psychology and their clinical applications. The dialogue then addressed the big human questions regarding values at the macrolevel and how we can bring about a balanced and harmonious life for all people, regardless of one's religious beliefs or background. In sharing a multitude of voices, we heard from politicians and economists and attained a perspective on art, social activism, the political implications of doing work on the ground, and how governance systems can be changed.

After gathering these multiple perspectives, I feel that we are just beginning to understand this complex sphere. If we were to now include the different perspectives from everyone else, we would start to get at the real complexity we are now facing in our daily world.

What would our world look like if we could listen to the heterogeneity of perspectives and different ways of being? Some people have data while others share heart quality. It is really about listening to what we have to say, and about coming out of the narrow silos of discipline that we are so often trapped in. It is beautiful when we can simply listen to other perspectives and allow them to be shared.

When I look at this kaleidoscope, and all its facets, I ask myself this: what is the common theme? It started with a clear understanding that this is not a purely academic dialogue. We are facing real, urgent problems. Johan Rockström presented this in a clear, scientific way, by showing us the facts: that in only 20 or 30 years, we have managed to destroy the very planet we are living from. Pauline Tangiora brought these facts into the hearts of all of us through her address. We heard from economists about the problems we have when facing poverty in the midst of plenty, the increasing inequality gap, and the growing difference between poor and rich in developed countries. On an individual level, we face a crisis of disconnection, of isolation, and of perceived loneliness, even though we are very connected through the Internet. All of these symptoms are realities, which we cannot deny. On the other hand, there was another theme coming through this kaleidoscope, which revealed an even stronger message: the message of hope. We heard about the concept of change and of plasticity. We learned how we are equipped with an array of motives that includes power, care, selfishness, altruism, and achievement, and that it is really up to us to balance out these motives and impulses. His Holiness said that it is our individual responsibility to step into our power to care, and this message came forward again and again with examples that this is possible on all levels. Gandhi once said, "You have to be the change you wish to see in the world." There is no other way. We also heard that we cannot put responsibility on politicians, the planet, or anything else. We also cannot give away our responsibility to holiness or to any kind of clergy. This will not do the job.

This dialogue also highlighted the media and the power and influence it would have if people would start to write—instead of about alarm, panic, fear, polarization, and segregation—about the power of care and altruism.

In the end, it only needs journalists writing about it because the facts are there anyway. But it is not only in our working places where we have the ability to effect change. We can also do this in our private spheres, with our children, family, and friends.

In closing, let us all look within our own spheres of power and expertise and put an intention into the power of care. If we can all do this together, we can achieve the dream and the vision His Holiness shared: that we move into a century of compassion. As His Holiness once said, "Compassion is not a luxury anymore. It is a necessity."

Inspiring Workshops

At the Power and Care conference, for the very first time, Mind & Life Europe offered eight workshops to deepen the participants' learning experience. This reflected Francisco Varela's wish from the very beginning: to use the Mind & Life platform to bring together third-person science with first-person inner experience, and match these forces into one.

Workshop 1: "Working with the Power-Oriented and Care-Taking Parts of Ourselves," led by Professor Richard Schwartz, offered participants the opportunity to identify their own tendencies toward power and care, and to see if these forces were in balance or not. He also shared how to enter a mindful and compassionate state, to create a greater balance and harmony with these forces.

Workshop 2: During "Awareness-Based Social Technologies for Social Change: What Does It Take to Lead from the Future as it Emerges," Martin Kalungu-Banda focused on teaching participants how to develop a new learning cycle to deal with current and emerging challenges by moving from an ego-system awareness, which cares about the well-being of *me*, to an eco-system awareness that cares about the well-being of all.

Workshop 3: Godfrey Spencer led "Practicing the Language of Nonviolent Communication." Developed by Marshall Rosenberg, this communication approach is based on the historical principles of nonviolence and works to listen to one's deeper needs and those of others for greater compassion and caring.

Workshop 4: In "The Art of the Fugue and the Art of Meditation," pianist Maria João Pires performed five preludes and fugues by J. S. Bach. Afterward, Buddhist monk Matthieu Ricard led short meditations on attentive presence, loving-kindness, compassion, celebration of goodness, equanimity, and pure awareness.

Workshop 5: "Experiencing Power and Care through Contemplative Practice across Traditions" was the topic led by Brother Thierry-Marie Courau, O.P., and Roshi Joan Halifax, Ph.D. It used inquiry, story, and contemplative practices from Buddhism and Catholicism to prepare the mind, the heart, and hands to integrate a principled and compassionate attitude toward power and care.

Workshops 6 and 7: These workshops both focused on "Caring about your Body and Mind." Rafael Ebner led a Yin Yoga session, which served to promote a sense of stillness and connection to the sensations inside, and the flow of energy through our system. Ryan Spielman took participants through an energizing Ashtanga Vinyasa Yoga series that created a gentle and dynamic moving meditation experience.

Workshop 8: In the last workshop, "Puppets: The Elusive Shift of Power and Care in Artistic Creation," Julian Crouch and Saskia Lane used live animation and puppetry techniques to explore the elusive and shifting balance of power and care as it relates to artistic creation.

Acknowledgments

Mind & Life Europe and the editors would like to thank the many people who helped to make the Power and Care conference and this book a reality.

We would like to thank His Holiness the Dalai Lama for his dedicated engagement to Mind & Life Europe. His wisdom, compassion, and teaching are a constant inspiration to us all. We wish to also extend our special thanks to Thupten Jinpa, for his extraordinary skill and dedication as a translator, as well as to Tseten Samdup Chhoekyapa and Tashi Phuntsok from the Office of His Holiness the Dalai Lama in Brussels.

We are very grateful for the wisdom, kindness, and generosity of our moderators, panel presenters, and workshop presenters who contributed their time to this event without any fees.

We offer deep thanks to Kate Karius for her dedicated guidance, persistence, and skill in bringing this book to life. Her work as a thoughtful researcher, writer, and editor of His Holiness the Dalai Lama and the contributors' texts proved vital to its successful completion.

The Power and Care event would not have been possible without the generous support of the following sponsors, for which Mind & Life Europe is very grateful: the L.B. Foundation, Switzerland; Renaud Samyn, Hong Kong; Maria Tussi Kluge, Germany; and the Hershey Family Foundation, United States. We additionally thank Mind & Life Europe's Gold and Silver sponsors for their crucial financial support.

We also wish to acknowledge Diego Hangartner, Mind & Life Europe's former managing director, and Arthur Zajonc, the former president of Mind & Life Institute. We especially thank the conference organizing team led by Conference Director Cornelius Pietzner, with Sander Tideman, Géraldine de Vries, Ute Brandes, Amy Cohen-Varela, Charles-Antoine Janssen, Ilios

Kotsou, Caroline Lesire, Nicole and Manoj Doods-Rauniar, Frans Goetghebeur, Hélène Goethals, Patrick Oliver, and Christine Moore. We thank all of the volunteers from Émergences, the staff of BOZAR, and the Social Neuroscience Department of the Max Planck Institute for Human Cognitive and Brain Science for their hard work and dedication to bringing this event to fruition.

We all hope that the wisdom, compassion, knowledge, and spirit of this book will be carried out into the world and bring happiness to all.

About Mind & Life Europe

Mind & Life Europe seeks to integrate contemplative wisdom and practices with contemporary science for investigating human experience and development. A number of programs are offered to support these goals:

European Summer Research Institute

The Mind & Life European Summer Research Institute (ESRI) serves to advance the training of a new generation of developmental scientists, cognitive/ affective neuroscientists, applied/clinical researchers, and contemplative scholar/practitioners. ESRI participants enter into dialogue with contemplative teachers and philosophers, as well as train in reflective practices, including meditation and yoga.

Communities of Practice

Each community of practice connects scientists, scholars, and professionals in the development of contemplative science. These communities cover both fundamental research and applied research and translate outcomes into regionally and nationally relevant frameworks that professionals and policy makers can put into action.

Francisco J. Varela Research Awards

Started in 2004, this career development award supports young scientists and scholars who are at the start of their careers in contemplative science research. The awards are granted to research programs that integrate first-person research methods with current cognitive, behavioral, physiological, clinical, or sociocultural research.

For more information on Mind & Life Europe, please visit
https://www.mindandlife-europe.org.

For more information on the Mind & Life Institute, please visit
https://www.mindandlife.org.

Contributors

Paul Collier is professor of economics and public policy at the Blavatnik School of Government, a professorial fellow of St Antony's College, and the founding director of the Centre for the Study of African Economies. From 1998 to 2003, Collier took a Public Service leave, during which he was director of the Research Development Department of the World Bank. He serves on the Economic Advisory Board of the International Finance Corporation and is a director of the International Growth Centre. His research covers the causes and consequences of civil war, the effects of aid, and the problems of democracy in low-income and natural-resources-rich societies. In 2014, Collier received a knighthood for services to promoting research and policy change in Africa.

Brother Thierry-Marie Courau, O.P., a French Dominican priest, is professor of theology of religions at the Institut Catholique de Paris in France. A former engineer and financial officer, he joined the Dominican Order in 1990. He presented a thesis in Catholic theology, focusing on the study of the three Bhavanakrama of Kamalashila, at the University of Strasbourg in France in 2004. After a year of travels in Buddhist regions, he began teaching at the Institut Catholique de Paris and became director of the Institute of Science and Theology of Religions, and then dean of the Theologicum. His publications focus on dialogue between irreducible singularities, Buddhism, religions, Christian salvation, and management. His latest book, *Les fontaines de l'éveil*, Paris, Cerf (The Fountains of Enlightenment), is a novel on Buddhist and Christian dialogue. Brother Thierry-Marie Courau is also president of the Conference of Catholic Theological Institutions of the International Federation of Catholic Universities and a member of the Council for Interreligious Relations of the Bishops' Conference of France. He is vice president of *Concilium: International Journal for Theology*.

Frans B. M. de Waal is a biologist and primatologist known for his work on the behavior and social intelligence of primates. His first book, *Chimpanzee Politics* (1982), compared the scheming of chimpanzees involved in power struggles with that of human politicians. De Waal draws parallels between primate and human behavior, from peacemaking and morality to culture. His scientific work has been published in hundreds of articles in journals such as *Science, Nature, Scientific American*, and outlets specialized in animal behavior. His latest books are *The Bonobo and the Atheist* (2013) and *Are We Smart Enough to Know How Smart Animals Are?* (2016). De Waal is C. H. Candler Professor in the Psychology Department of Emory University and director of the Living Links Center at the Yerkes National Primate Research Center in Atlanta, Georgia. He has been elected to the National Academy of Sciences (USA), the American Academy of Arts and Sciences, and the Royal Dutch Academy of Sciences.

Olafur Eliasson, born in 1967, works in a wide range of media, including installation, painting, sculpture, and photography. Since 1997, his critically acclaimed solo shows have appeared in major museums around the world, such as the Museum of Modern Art, New York; Tate Modern, London; and the Venice Biennale. Eliasson's projects in public spaces include The New York City Waterfalls, 2008, and Cirkelbroen (The Circle Bridge), Copenhagen, Denmark, 2015. Established in 1995, his Berlin studio numbers today about 90 craftspersons, specialized technicians, architects, archivists, administrators, and cooks. In July 2011, Eliasson hosted the seminar "How to Train Compassion," conceived and developed by social neuroscientist Tania Singer, at his studio in Berlin. Eliasson is the head of Studio Other Spaces, an international office for art and architecture established with architect Sebastian Behmann in 2014, and Little Sun, a social business that produces the Little Sun solar lamp for use in off-grid communities and spreads awareness about the need to expand access to sustainable energy to all.

Scilla Elworthy, Ph.D., founded the Oxford Research Group in 1982 to develop effective dialogue between nuclear weapons policy makers worldwide and their critics, including a series of dialogues between Chinese, Russian, and Western nuclear scientists and the military, for which she has been three times nominated for the Nobel Peace Prize. She founded Peace Direct in 2002 to fund, promote, and learn from local peace builders in conflict areas; it was voted Best New Charity in 2005. Scilla was awarded the Niwano Peace Prize in 2003 and was adviser to Peter Gabriel, Archbishop Desmond Tutu, and Sir Richard Branson in setting up "The Elders." She cofounded Rising Women Rising World in 2013 and FemmeQ in 2016. She advises the leadership of selected international corporations and teaches young social entrepreneurs; her latest book is *Peace Is Now Possible: The Business Plan to Build a World without War*, and her TED Talk on nonviolence has been viewed by over 1,130,000 people.

Alexandra M. Freund is a professor of psychology at the University of Zurich in Switzerland. She studied psychology at the University of Heidelberg and the Free University Berlin, where she also received her Ph.D. She was a postdoctoral fellow at Stanford University and returned to Germany to codirect a project on developmental regulation with Paul B. Baltes at the Max Planck Institute for Human Development in Berlin for seven years. After that, she was an assistant professor and later an associate professor at Northwestern University. Since 2005, she has been a full professor at the University of Zurich. Alexandra M. Freund was elected a founding member of the Young Academy of Sciences. In 2013, she received a mentoring award, in 2015, she received the Humboldt Research Award, and in 2017 she was elected a member of the Wilhelm Wundt Society. Since 2010, she has been associate editor of the American Psychological Association journal *Psychology and Aging*. Central research interests are successful aging, developmental regulation, and motivation across the life span.

Tenzin Gyatso, His Holiness the Dalai Lama, was born on July 6, 1935, in a small village called Taktser in northeastern Tibet. Born to a peasant family, he was recognized at the age of two as the Buddha of Compassion, who chose to reincarnate for the purpose of serving human beings. Winner of the Nobel Prize for Peace in 1989, he is universally respected as a spokesperson for the compassionate and peaceful resolution of human conflict. He has traveled extensively, speaking on subjects including universal responsibility, love, compassion, and kindness. He also has a vigorous interest in learning the newest developments in science, and he brings to bear both a voice for the humanistic implications of the findings and a high degree of intuitive methodological sophistication. He is a cofounder of the Mind & Life Institute.

Markus Heinrichs studied psychology at the University of Wurzburg and the University of Bonn and received his Ph.D. from the University of Trier in Germany. After a postdoctoral fellowship at the University of Zurich in Switzerland, he was an assistant professor of clinical psychology and psychobiology at the University of Zurich. Since 2009, Heinrichs has been chair of the Department of Psychology and professor of biological and personality psychology at the University of Freiburg in Germany. Since 2010, he has headed the Social Neuroscience Research Group at the Freiburg Brain Imaging Center and has directed the Outpatient Clinic for Stress-Related Disorders. He has pioneered a new field, demonstrating that the neurohormone oxytocin is a key mediator in the regulation of human social cognition and behavior and establishing oxytocin as a target for novel treatment approaches.

Sarah Blaffer Hrdy is an evolutionary anthropologist and professor emerita at the University of California, Davis. She is a former Guggenheim fellow elected to the National Academy of Sciences (USA), the American Academy of Arts and Sciences, the California Academy of Sciences, and the American Philosophical Society. Her books include *The Langurs of Abu: Female and Male Strategies of Reproduction*; *The Woman That Never Evolved*; *Mother Nature*; and most recently, *Mothers and Others: The Evolutionary Origins of Mutual Understanding*, an exploration of the cognitive and emotional implications of humankind's long legacy of shared child-rearing, which received both the 2012 J. I. Staley Prize from the School of Advanced Research and the Howells Prize at the American Anthropological Association. In 2014, she was awarded the National Academy of Sciences award for scientific reviewing. A mother and grandmother, she lives in Northern California, where she and her husband, Dan, combine habitat restoration with growing walnuts.

Thupten Jinpa, Ph.D., holds a Geshe Lharam degree from the Shartse College of Ganden Monastic University, South India, as well as a B.A. Honors in Philosophy and a Ph.D. in Religious Studies from Cambridge University. Jinpa has been the principal English translator to His Holiness the Dalai Lama since 1985 and has translated and edited numerous books by the Dalai Lama, including *The New York Times'* best seller *Ethics for the New Millennium*. His own publications include numerous works in Tibetan and English and translations of major Tibetan works. His latest book is *A Fearless Heart: How the Courage to be Compassionate Can Transform Our Lives*. He is the main author of CCT (Compassion Cultivation Training), an eight-week formal program developed at the Center for Compassion and Altruism Research and Education at Stanford University. Jinpa is an adjunct professor at the Faculty of Religious Studies at McGill University, the founder and president of the Institute of Tibetan Classics, and the chairman of the board of the Mind & Life Institute.

Frédéric Laloux is a former associate partner with McKinsey & Company. He holds an MBA from INSEAD and a degree in coaching from Newfield Network in Boulder, Colorado. He has traveled widely and speaks five languages fluently. Laloux works as an adviser, coach, and facilitator for corporate leaders who feel called to explore fundamentally new ways of organizing. His work draws on two strands: first, his deep understanding of the inner workings of organizations, and, second, his long-standing fascination with the topic of human development and his own joyful journey of personal and spiritual growth. His research in the field of emerging organizational models, published in his book *Reinventing Organizations*, has been described as "groundbreaking" and "a leap in management thinking" by some of the most respected scholars in the field of human development and management. The book focuses on how a currently emerging, new form of consciousness is bringing forth a radically more soulful, purposeful, and productive management paradigm.

Alaa Murabit, M.D., founded The Voice of Libyan Women in 2011 at the age of 21. With a strong focus on challenging societal and cultural norms and utilizing traditional and historical role models, Murabit champions women's participation in peace processes and conflict mediation. Her programs, such as the groundbreaking Noor Campaign, are replicated internationally. Murabit acts as advisor to numerous international security boards, think tanks, and organizations. She was nominated to the UN Security Council resolution 1325 (Women, Peace, and Security) Global Advisory Board, to the UN Women Global Advisory Board, and to Harvard University's Everywoman, Everywhere initiative. In March 2015, Murabit was selected as the inaugural civil society speaker at the official Commission on the Status of Women opening session. Murabit's TED Talk, released in July 2015, "What My Religion Really Says about Women," was selected as the TED Talk of the Day and one of four moving TED Talks you should watch right now by *The New York Times*.

Matthieu Ricard, Ph.D., is a Buddhist monk at Shechen Monastery in Nepal. He received a Ph.D. in cell genetics at the Institut Pasteur in France under Nobel Laureate

François Jacob. He has lived in the Himalayas since 1972, studying with Kangyur Rinpoche and Dilgo Khyentse Rinpoche, two respected Tibetan spiritual masters. Since 1989, he has served as French interpreter for His Holiness the Dalai Lama. He is the author of *The Monk and the Philosopher* (with his father, French thinker Jean-François Revel); *The Quantum and the Lotus* (with astrophysicist Trinh Xuan Thuan); *Happiness*; *Why Meditate?*; *Altruism*; *Beyond the Self* (with neuroscientist Wolf Singer); and *In Search of Wisdom* (with psychiatrist Christophe André and philosopher Alexandre Jollien). He has translated several books from Tibetan, including *The Life of Shabkar* and *Enlightened Vagabond*. As a photographer, he has published numerous albums, including *The Spirit of Tibet* and *Motionless Journey*. He donates all proceeds from his books to 200 humanitarian projects in Tibet, Nepal, and India, through his humanitarian association Karuna-Shechen.

Johan Rockström is a professor in environmental science with emphasis on water resources and global sustainability at Stockholm University and the executive director of the Stockholm Resilience Centre. He is an internationally recognized scientist on global sustainability issues. He led the recent development of the new Planetary Boundaries framework for human development in the current era of rapid global change. He is a leading scientist on global water resources and strategies to build resilience in water scarce regions of the world, with more than 15 years' experience from applied water research in tropical regions and more than 100 research publications in fields ranging from applied land and water management to global sustainability. He serves on several scientific committees and boards. He is vice chair of the science advisory board of the Potsdam Institute for Climate Impact Research.

Richard Schwartz, Ph.D., is on the faculty of the Department of Psychiatry at Harvard University. He developed the Internal Family Systems (IFS) model of psychotherapy in response to clients' descriptions of various extreme "parts" or subpersonalities within themselves. He used his background as a systems-oriented family therapist to understand and change these inner networks of parts in clients. He also discovered that when clients' parts relaxed, a state he called the Self would emerge spontaneously, and when in that state, clients related to themselves with compassion and confidence that would help their parts transform. While designed as an approach to psychotherapy, IFS has expanded to inform a wide variety of contemplative practices and spiritual traditions and is used for conflict resolution. It is taught throughout the United States, Europe, and Israel. Schwartz lives in Brookline, Massachusetts.

Tania Singer has been a professor and director of the Max Planck Institute for Human Cognitive and Brain Sciences in Leipzig, Germany, since 2010. After completing her Ph.D. in psychology at the Max Planck Institute for Human Development in Berlin, she became a postdoctoral fellow at the Wellcome Department of Imaging Neuroscience at UCL and at the Institute of Cognitive Neuroscience in London. In 2006, she joined the University of Zurich as assistant professor and later became codirector of the Laboratory for Social and Neural Systems Research. Her research focuses on the foundations of human social behavior and on the neuronal, developmental, and hormonal mechanisms underlying social cognition and emotions. She investigates the psychological and neuroscientific longitudinal effects of compassion and mental training on subjective well-being, brain, mind and social understanding, health, and cooperation (The ReSource Project). Further, she collaborates with Professor Dennis J. Snower from the Kiel Institute for the World Economy on the topic of Caring Economics, focusing on how biology and psychology can inform new economic models.

Dennis J. Snower is president of the Kiel Institute for the World Economy and professor of economics at the Christian-Albrechts University of Kiel in Germany. He is president of the Global Economic Symposium and the Global Solutions Initiative. He is also a research fellow at the Center for Economic Policy Research (London), IZA (Institute for the Future of Work, Bonn), and CESifo (Munich). Snower earned a B.A. and M.A. from New College, Oxford University, and an M.A. and a Ph.D. from Princeton University. He is an expert on labor economics, public policy, and inflation–unemployment trade-offs. As part of his research career, he originated the "insider–outsider" theory of employment and unemployment with Assar Lindbeck, the theory of "high–low search" with Steve Alpern, and the "chain reaction theory of unemployment" and the theory of "frictional growth" with Marika Karanassou and Hector Sala. He has been a visiting professor at many universities around the world and has advised a variety of international organizations and national governments on macroeconomic policy, employment policy, and welfare state policy.

Rabbi Awraham Soetendorp is an award-winning human rights advocate, lecturer, writer, environmental activist, and champion of civil society worldwide. Born in 1943 in Amsterdam, the Netherlands, Rabbi Soetendorp was saved by a righteous couple. He received his ordination from Leo Baeck College of London in 1967 and was instrumental in the reestablishment of Jewish communities in the Netherlands. Rabbi Soetendorp is the founder and president of the Jacob Soetendorp Institute for Human Values in the Netherlands, a founding member of Green Cross International, and the founder and chair of the Day of Respect Foundation as well as the Hope for Children Fund. He serves as an Earth Charter commissioner and a Millennium Development ambassador and is a founding member of the Islam and the West Dialogue Group of the World Economic Forum. He has received the Peace Builders Award from the Alliance for International Conflict Prevention and Resolution and the "Peace Through Dialogue" Interfaith Gold Medallion from the International Council of Christians and Jews.

Theo Sowa is an independent advisor and consultant, specializing in international social development with a particular emphasis on rights and protection issues. She is currently the CEO of the African Women's Development Fund. Her work includes advisory roles to African and other international women and children's rights activists and leaders, plus policy development and advocacy with a variety of international agencies and organizations. Sowa is a trustee of Comic Relief (and chair of Comic Relief's International Grants Committee), a member of the African Advisory Board of the Stephen Lewis Foundation, a patron of Evidence for Development, a board member of the UBS Optimus Foundation, and a board member of the Graça Machel Trust. She has authored many publications, including being a contributing editor to *The Impact of War on Children*, a contributing author and coeditor of a Harvard Law School/UNICEF Innocenti publication on "Children and Transitional Justice," and coauthor of *Groupwork and Intermediate Treatment*.

Pauline Tangiora, J.P., Q.S.O., Q.S.M., is a Maori elder from the Rongomaiwahine Tribe on the East Coast of the North Island of Aotearoa, New Zealand. She also has affiliations to many other tribes. She is a justice of the peace, a former president and currently vice president and life member of the Women's International League for Peace and Freedom Aotearoa, the former regional women's representative for the World Council for Indigenous Peoples, and a former Earth Charter commissioner. She is currently an ambassador to the Earth Council International, kuia (elder) for the Eastern Institute of Technology Hawkes Bay, an elder to the Disarmament and Security Centre Otautahi, the past chairperson of Te Whanau o Rongomaiwahine Trust, a life member of the Maori Women's Welfare League, a patroness of the Peace Foundation, an honorary board member to One Earth Institute, a founding and current member of the World Future Council, and an ambassador to The International Council for Thirteen Indigenous Grandmothers Council. She has represented Aotearoa at many international fora and was a consultant to the International Steering Committee of the World Court Project.

Jody Williams is an American political activist who received the Nobel Peace Prize in 1997. She and the organization she helped found in 1992, the International Campaign to Ban Landmines, shared the prize for their groundbreaking work leading to the Mine Ban Treaty that year. An outspoken peace activist since the Vietnam War, she struggles to reclaim the real meaning of peace, which is defined by human security, not national security. For her, working for peace requires dogged persistence and a commitment to sustainable peace, built on environmental justice and meeting the basic needs of the majority of people on our planet. Since January of 2006, Williams has worked toward those ends through the Nobel Women's Initiative, which she chairs. Mairead Maguire (Northern Ireland), Rigoberta Menchú Tum (Guatemala), Shirin Ebadi (Iran), Leymah Gbowee (Liberia), and Tawakkol Karman (Yemen) are the other members of the initiative. Using the prestige of the Nobel Peace Prize and the influence and access of the women Nobel Laureates, the Nobel Women's Initiative works to support and amplify the efforts of women around the world working for sustainable peace with justice and equality.

Index

Karius, Kate, 183
Kill, to, 5, 24, 32, 43, 77, 83, 98–100,
    102–103, 141–143, 161–164
Killer monks, 100
Kin, 19, 122–123
King, Martin Luther, Jr., xi, 52, 75
Knowledge, ancient, 3–4, 5n1
Koran, the. *See* Islam

Laloux, Frédéric, 151, 165–170, 174
Leadership, 11, 75, 114–115, 143
Lenin, 127
LGBTQQIA people, 140
Listening, 43, 76, 105–107, 141, 145,
    161–163, 168, 178
Living organisms, 166, 168. *See also*
    Systems
Lola ya Bonobo Sanctuary, 9–10
Love
  inability to feel, 82, 85
  for our planet and Mother Earth,
    115
  the practice of love and compassion 5,
    12, 13, 43, 80–83, 147, 149, 174
  religion is, 89–90, 91
  of the stranger, 125
Loving-kindness
  Buddhist approach to opening the
    heart, 82–84
  effect of practices to open the heart in
    The ReSource Project, 65, 68, 71
  for everyone, 103, 105–107
  well-being of the self-and others,
    73n2, 83, 121, 177

Machines. *See* Mechanistic view
Male dominance, 7, 114–115
Mandela, Nelson, 162–163
Marxism, 126, 127
Material development. *See* Happiness
Mauri, 93–94, 96n1
Mechanistic view, 166, 168
Médecins Sans Frontières (MSF), 136

Media, 148, 179
Meditation
  goal of, 83–86
  training programs, 63–73
Mentalizing. *See* Theory of Mind
Metta-meditation. *See* Loving-kindness
Mind & Life Dialogues, 3, 4
Mind, the. *See also* Brain, the
  and ancient Indian knowledge, 3–4
  and attachment, 82–83, 97, 100, 174
  and dealing with emotions, 82
  human-made problems of the, 13,
    149, 175
  Theory of Mind, 20–21, 68–70
  training in mindfulness, 64, 67–68,
    76–78
  using intelligence to cultivate a com-
    passionate attitude towards others,
    22, 24, 43, 65–70, 149, 174–175
Mindfulness
  cultivating through body-scan and
    breathing meditation practices in
    The ReSource Project, 64, 67–68
  and extreme emotions, 76–78
Minorities, 98, 111
Modern technology, 3, 25, 95, 114
Money
  fair distribution of, 81
  giving and taking, 71–73, 143–144,
    145–145, 162–164
  and the global economy, 131–132
  investing, 135–136
  and motives of self-interest, care, and
    power, 121–122
  wages, 134
Montreal Protocol, 43
Mother Earth, 93, 115
Mothers, 9–11, 15–25, 77, 84, 87, 93–96,
    101, 109, 115, 135, 149
Motivation and motives, 7, 49–50, 66,
    71–72, 82, 97, 121–129
Muhammad, 91, 149. *See also* Islam
Multinational company, 95